THE DANCE OF DIFFERENCE
BOOK I

THE NEW FRONTIER
OF
SEXUAL ORIENTATION

LEARNING TO VALUE OUR COMMON HUMANITY

SHIRLEY ANDERSON
FLETCHER

www.danceofdifference.com

Pearson Publishing
P.O. Box 341264
Bethesda, MD. 20827

©2010 by Shirley Anderson Fletcher

All rights reserved. No part of this book may be reproduced in any form or by any means, electronic or mechanical, including photocopying, recording, or by any information storage and retrieval system or otherwise (quotations of three hundred words or less excepted) without permission in writing from the publisher.

Cover design by Rebecca Dodelin

ISBN-10: 1453793445
EAN-13: 9781453793442

TO ALL WHO STRUGGLE FOR
SOCIAL JUSTICE

TABLE OF CONTENTS

INTRODUCTION ix

Chapter 1 1
Sexual Orientation And Heterosexism—One Human Family

Chapter 2 9
Learning to Fear, Yet Making Progress

Chapter 3 17
Dialogue: Building Understanding and Connection

Chapter 4 55
Closing Reflections

Appendix A 71
Common Scenarios—Ten Possible Responses for Concerned Heterosexuals

Appendix B
Stories of Prejudice and Discrimination 79

Endnotes 103

ACKNOWLEDGMENTS

My learning about the personal and institutional impact of heterosexism, racism and sexism increased significantly because of my membership in the consulting network of Elsie Y. Cross Associates, Inc. I have grown in awareness and skill because of competent colleagues and committed clients who have also supported me in my writing. Dr. Kathy Obear, Bo Razak, Mark Kaplan, Heather Wishik, Rushton Paul Jr. and Dr. Roger Karsk reviewed my manuscript and gave invaluable feedback. The model 'Dialogue with Difference' developed by Dr. Delyte Frost has helped me personally to connect across difference as it has helped my clients. I am deeply grateful to the Rev. Dr. Jamie Washington for our candid dialogue about what it is like to be gay. Tom Finn has generously shared his experience of writing and publishing, as well as his considerable resources. My son Douglas Fletcher and daughter in law Kendra Williams Fletcher pored over early manuscripts, and gave insightful feedback and encouragement. From the outset, my sister Beverley Anderson Manley insisted that I had something important to offer in my writing. John Vaillant advised me early in the process to write from my unique experience as a black woman who grew up in the homophobic culture of Jamaica and immigrated to the United States as an adult. My writing coach Yvette Hyater-Adams not only helped me to develop my craft as a writer, but she never faltered in her belief that my trilogy of books would be a useful contribution to the literature about issues of oppression. Finally I thank my husband Richard for stimulating conversations about our need as human beings to denigrate 'the different other.' I am also very grateful that he took over the management of our household so that I could focus on my writing.

INTRODUCTION

I am a black, heterosexual grandmother. I was born in Jamaica and grew up there in the 1940s and '50s. Like many innocent children all over the world, I started to learn from an early age to fear people who were lesbian, gay, or bisexual. Adults around me spat the word "homosexual"' out with such venom it made me shiver. Simultaneously, I was learning that heterosexuals were somehow morally superior to people who were homosexual. I am embarrassed to admit it, but for most of my life I have been in denial that discrimination against lesbian, gay, and bisexual people was an issue that I needed to be concerned about. However, after years of struggling with my deeply embedded prejudices and biases, I have become an active ally in the movement for human rights and social justice for lesbian, gay, and bisexual people.

How was I able to move out of denial? One key factor was that I was passionate about my anti-sexism and anti-racism work. It took me a while, but I finally figured out that oppression based on sexism, racism, anti-Semitism, or classism is really no different than oppression based on heterosexism, i.e., the oppression of people who are or are assumed to be gay, lesbian, or bisexual. All are based on beliefs of superiority of one group over another. All involve the degradation and exploitation of one group by another. All reject the full humanity of the group that is perceived to be inferior.

My personal challenges with my own homophobia—i.e., my discomfort, fear, or hatred of people who are or are assumed to be lesbian, gay, or bisexual—and my concerns about my grandchildren and other youngsters growing up in a homophobic world are central to my story. In Appendix A, I describe common scenarios of prejudice and discrimination against people who are lesbian, gay, and bisexual (LGBs). For heterosexuals who want to make a difference, I offer ways of responding to these scenarios. It is true that many LGB people have carved out productive and successful lives despite the fact that they are treated like second-class citizens legally and socially. The stories in Appendix B, however, offer a glimpse into the challenges meted out to LGB people on a day-to-day basis by heterosexuals, intentionally or unintentionally. These are true stories of incidents of bias and discrimination that occurred in corporate America and in communities around the country. The victims of these incidents told me their stories. In some instances, I witnessed the incident myself. I have of course changed the names of people in these stories in order to preserve confidentiality. The reader will observe that the stories cut across race, religion, gender, age, and social/economic class as well as hierarchical levels in organizations.

This exploration of the impact of sexual orientation, a term used to describe one's primary sexual attraction to another, is the first in a trilogy of books about prejudice and discrimination based on identity. The remaining books focus on race and gender. The overarching theoretical framework for the trilogy is the concept of dominant and subordinated group membership. This concept, which colleagues and I have applied to our work on issues of diversity for a couple of decades, recognizes the existence of socially constructed hierarchies based on identity. Membership in a dominant or subordinated group determines to a large degree how one is perceived and how one is treated. Ultimately dominant groups have power

INTRODUCTION

over groups that are subordinated. Depending on group membership, our sexual orientation, our race, or our gender can expand our potential or severely limit access and opportunities. Throughout this text on sexual orientation, I refer to heterosexuals, the group that perceives itself to be superior, as the dominant group. In this societal paradigm of superiority/inferiority, people who are homosexual are defined as the subordinated group. It is important to note that individual heterosexuals may be unconscious or unaware of their impact on the lives of LGB people and, they may not perceive themselves to be superior. Nevertheless, this belief in the superiority of heterosexuals is visible globally in our attitudes, our actions, and our laws as well as in our social behavior. I elaborate on the meaning of this complex concept as the chapters unfold.

Although transgender is not a sexual orientation, this subordinated group has formed an alliance with lesbian, gay, and bisexual people in their mutual struggle for equality. Therefore, I use the inclusive terminology "LGBT" as I describe issues of prejudice and discrimination. I provide statistics on violence against the LGBT community and also point to progress towards equal rights, slow though it may be, in Jamaica, the United States, Europe, and other countries. Issues of gender identity and gender expression that are specific to the transgender community are explored in my soon-to-be-published book on gender.

I am an applied behavioral scientist with thirty years of experience consulting to corporations and government agencies in the United States and Europe on the impact of prejudice and discrimination in the work environment. My experience has taught me that the ability to dialogue and really hear without judgment the experience of someone with a different identity significantly expands awareness and understanding. As a result, I have included in each of these books a spontaneous dialogue about the topic under exploration. These dialogues are based on a methodology developed by our colleague Delyte Frost, Ph.D. In Chapter 3 of this book, I have a dialogue with the Rev. Dr. Jamie Washington, a gay African American colleague, about the impact and implications of being gay in a world that defines people who are lesbian, gay, and bisexual as inferior because of their sexual orientation. Jamie talks freely and openly about the devastating impact of homophobia within the black community, and about the self-hatred that mars the lives of people who are homosexual regardless of race. In the process he also describes the tragic impact of AIDS in the African American community. As I listen to Jamie, I have the sense that we live in two different worlds. His sexual orientation has presented him with innumerable challenges. My sexual orientation, on the other hand, has never been an obstacle in my personal life or in my career.

As our dialogue unfolds, Jamie shares the painful isolation of black gays and lesbians who are simultaneously rejected by their own families, as well as by the race prejudice of the white homosexual community. He also speaks about the impact on the gay community of the complex interrelationships of socioeconomic class, religion, gender, and sexual orientation.

This series of books is for anyone who is curious or concerned about the personal and societal dynamics of difference based on identity. I found out early in my work on issues of diversity and inclusion that I could neither teach nor learn without my self being fully involved. In other words, these are not subjects that we can hold at arm's length. The self is at the center of this type of exploration and learning. And it takes courage to uncover our own prejudices and fears. It takes courage to speak out against discrimination. It takes courage to stay compassionate in the face of bigotry. When

I'm having a discussion about or reading about gender, I am instantly involved because of my personal experience of being a woman and my knowledge about what life is like for women in my family, for women colleagues and friends, as well as for women in general. When the discussion turns to race or sexual orientation, or nationality, the same thing applies. My thoughts, my emotions, and my values are triggered because I have had many positive as well as many negative experiences of being a woman, being black, and being an immigrant.

As you read, you may notice that some powerful feelings are being evoked. I expect that you may embrace or outright reject some of what is presented here. This is all part of the process of dealing with these issues that are so complex and controversial, yet to a degree so familiar. It is possible that deeper insights and understanding will emerge because you are intimately engaged with the material presented. You may also be able to connect what you are reading to your own experience, as well as to your own observations of how people relate to each other within their own identity groups, or with others who are different. My hope is that you will be encouraged to have dialogues about these issues of difference with people who are like you as well as with people who are different from you. We can choose to be open and curious about the "different other," or we can choose to have a limited or skewed understanding of the realities and challenges of groups that are subordinated. We can also choose to be lifelong learners and, in the process, become more deeply aware of our common humanity.

CHAPTER 1

SEXUAL ORIENTATION AND HETEROSEXISM

ONE HUMAN FAMILY

I was about seven years old when I overheard my gentle, churchgoing father say to a friend, "Those men are an abomination. They should all be killed!" Waves of shock went through my body. How could my father say something so awful? Who were these men? What could they have done to make my father so angry? I didn't understand until years later that he was talking about men who were gay. The moment stayed with me because the venom and hostility in his voice was unmistakable and frightening. I didn't know it at the time, but that was the opening shot in my negative programming regarding homosexuality, the emotional, romantic, and sexual attraction to members of the same sex. My father was expressing fear and hatred of gay men.

We in the Western world rightly take pride in the fact that we are freedom-loving people. This is particularly true of us Americans. We have witnessed and participated in the falling of gender barriers and race barriers, and we have grown in our humanity as a result. Yet many of us continue to fiercely resist the liberation of the group we have subordinated because of their sexual orientation. This continues even though our mothers and fathers, our sisters and our brothers, our sons and daughters are the members of this group that is the target of our prejudice and bigotry.

Whether we are black or white, Muslim, Jew, or Christian, upper class, middle class, or poor, we are somehow able to tolerate the intolerable. Will the expansion in our consciousness regarding race and gender oppression provide the spiritual fuel for breaking through the frontiers of homophobia[1] and heterosexism?[2]

As I reflect on the impact of the term "sexual orientation,"[3] I am reminded that so many of us who are heterosexual[4] seem to focus only on the issue of sexuality when the conversation is about gays[5] and lesbians.[6] However, we typically perceive heterosexuals holistically, and we don't define heterosexuals by their sex lives only. Somehow it is hard for us to accept that gays, lesbians, and bisexuals[7] are fully functional human beings with ordinary lives just like heterosexuals. Like us, gays, lesbians, and bisexuals are managing careers, raising children, gardening, looking after pets, worrying about taxes, and wondering if they will get all of their tasks done. Same-sex couples have told me that expressions of sexual intimacy are often the last item on their personal list of shared activities and interests.

As a heterosexual myself, I am aware that we typically believe that heterosexuality is the only normal and healthy sexual orientation. In the dominant heterosexual world that we have created, this means that no other valid sexual orientation exists. Anything different from heterosexuality is therefore deviant. It is the result of sinful, evil, and willful behavior. Many of us then conclude that we have no responsibility for the hatred and violence that is perpetrated against homosexuals. Neither are we responsible for the withholding of civil rights from people who identify as lesbian, gay, or bisexual. We believe that people who are gay, lesbian, or bisexual could act like "normal people" if they so choose. What I am describing here is a pattern of beliefs expressed by many heterosexuals. These are not necessarily the belief system of every heterosexual!

Over the years, I've encountered many adult heterosexuals who have said, "I didn't even know that I had a sexual orientation. I thought it was only gays and lesbians who did." I must confess that until I started to learn about these issues professionally, I also did not know that I had a sexual orientation. I just never thought about it, and as I was growing up I don't remember any references by adults to my sexual orientation, or to my developing sexual identity. Dominant group members are the "norm," so we define things based on how they differ from this perceived norm. As organization consultant and author Carol Pierce notes:

> It is hard even to focus on how dominance is associated with identifying as heterosexual. Heterosexuality is so normal that having to think through how we acquired attributes of heterosexuality, much less that it is allied with dominance, seems like nit picking, ridiculous, and a waste of time. Our resistance is so deep that the topic seems a non-subject. We are more used to identifying dominant or subordinate in terms of male/female issues and people of color/white people concerns.[8]

In a world that is dominated by heterosexuals, this profound silence about sexual orientation should not be surprising. As I was growing up, silence about sexual orientation was deafening. Silence about the diversity of sexual orientation has been the norm for decades. This is certainly true for people of my generation who grew up in the '40s and '50s. I am still amazed that I remained clueless about the existence of gays, lesbians, and bisexuals until I entered my thirties. It wasn't until I was in my fifties that I discovered that one of my uncles had a son who was gay and who died of AIDS. I never met him. I assume that some family members must have known of this young man's existence. However, no one said a word. There has been a conspiracy of silence across generations that has rendered gays, lesbians, and bisexuals invisible. I am ashamed to admit that families, including my own, and social institutions, including churches, mosques, synagogues, schools, and the judicial/legal system, participated in this conspiracy of silence.

The United States military actually formalized this requirement for silence and invisibility with its "Don't Ask, Don't Tell" policy. One result of institutional silence is that it gives free reign to bigots to harass and intimidate lesbians, gays, and bisexuals as well as people who are transgender. Harassers of people who are lesbian, gay, bisexual, and transgender (LGBTs) know that for the most part, they are safe from punishment because the fear of losing jobs coupled with the fear of losing the respect of colleagues and friends will likely keep LGBT people silent.

My colleague Mark Kaplan[9] has named the process I am describing as *"the Cycle of Invisibility that so insidiously inhibits progress on the issue."* He reminds us that many heterosexuals believe that being gay is not so bad because LGBT people can easily hide their sexual orientation. Some years ago, a young Latino man shared with me the pain and complexities involved in hiding the fact that he is gay. He said:

> I am an outgoing, friendly person, and I have always felt uncomfortable about the fact that I have hidden my sexual orientation from everyone. I worry every day that I may inadvertently say or do something that will "out" me at work or in my family. I finally decided to come out to my

boss, because he's been so supportive of my development, and I felt that I could trust the company's anti-discrimination policy. I also want to be honest about who I am. But I still haven't come out to my co-workers.

Imagine my amazement when he subsequently came out in a company workshop that I was facilitating. In conversation with him afterwards, I started to grasp the fact that coming out is an ongoing process, that it can be convoluted and seemingly irrational. It seems that if you are gay, bisexual, lesbian or transgender, there are some key questions that are never far from your mind. Is it safe for me to come out? Can I trust that my family will continue to love me if I tell them that I am a lesbian? Would it be a career-limiting mistake for me to come out in my organization? How can I maintain my sanity while constantly weighing the risks of secrecy vs. openness?

On the other hand, those of us who are heterosexual flaunt our sexual orientation daily. And, more often than not, we are completely unaware of it. But the wedding rings we wear, pictures of loved ones on our desks at work, daily conversations about our spouses, and the freedom to invite loved ones to social events at work or to introduce our spouses to friends and neighbors are just a few examples of the visibility of heterosexuality. We also send messages to LGBT people that they better stay closeted. So are statements at work that include, "Why is sexual orientation included in our diversity work? We shouldn't be talking about sex at work" and "We are doing enough with workshops on race and gender—do we really have to add sexual orientation to the mix?" In social settings I have heard presumed heterosexuals say, "I don't approve of the homosexual lifestyle." "They should stop flaunting their sexual orientation." "I saw two of them kissing on TV and I thought I was going to be sick." I imagine that we are all familiar with the laughter that greets so-called "gay jokes" at work and in social settings.

As heterosexuals, we have found multiple ways to communicate to people who are lesbian, gay, or bisexual that this is a heterosexual world and we mean to keep it that way. Physical attack, including murder, is a clear message.

The insidiousness of the *"Cycle of Invisibility"* is that it not only keeps LGBT people "in their place" but it also undermines the struggle for equality and social justice. The choice for LGBT people is to stay closeted and thereby collude in maintaining the *"Cycle of Invisibility"* or to take the risk of coming out, thereby breaking the cycle and furthering the cause for human rights.

We may never know the full extent of the harm this societal requirement for silence and invisibility has inflicted on family members, on friends, or on our organizations and communities. My personal and professional experience supports Carol Pierce's observation that:

> …even though many of us may privately question cultural assumptions about homosexuality, few straight people stand up publicly in defense of gay rights. We remain quiet as a group, thus supporting all the ways the silences around homosexuality are built into our culture. This silence is like a cultural mask behind which no one must speak openly about homosexuality.[10]

On the occasions when I find the courage to speak up on the issue of LGBT rights in family gatherings or with friends, the result is often an awkward silence, or a heated exchange. *"Shirley, what is wrong with you?"* is too frequently the opening shot when folks respond to me. In organizations where I've consulted on issues of sexual orientation, I've been dismayed by the public silence of employees who have told me privately that they are concerned about prejudice and discrimination against gays, lesbians, and bisexuals. Many have said to me, *"It's easy for you to say that I should speak up. You don't work here. If I speak up, I won't be seen as a team player. My career would be in jeopardy."* Not surprisingly, the culture of the organization reflects the culture of the society.

In the United States, this intergenerational silence and invisibility was broken with the Stonewall riot that began on June 28, 1969, and lasted for two days. This protest against police harassment of LGBT people at the Stonewall Inn in New York's West Village signaled the start of the modern gay rights movement. In subsequent decades, increasing numbers of LGBT people have come out of the closet[11] and publicly joined the struggle for human rights.

Despite the fact that homophobia is still a significant barrier in Europe, LGBT people, with the support of heterosexual allies, are experiencing the dismantling of legal and societal taboos in countries like the United Kingdom and the Netherlands. Countries that sanction same-sex marriage include Canada, Denmark, Norway, Sweden, Spain, Iceland, Finland, the Netherlands, Belgium, Great Britain, France, Luxembourg, Argentina, New Zealand, and South Africa. Here in the United States, however, gay marriage is currently legal only in Massachusetts, New Hampshire, Connecticut, Iowa, Vermont, and the District of Columbia.[12] In the last decade in the Caribbean and Latin America, gays, lesbians, and bisexuals have been risking their lives as they initiate their struggle for equal rights.

According to Human Rights Watch's International Gay and Lesbian Human Rights Commission, gay and lesbian people risk punishment by death in Iran, Saudi Arabia, United Arab Emirates, Yemen, Mauritania, and parts of Nigeria and Sudan. The commission also states that sanctions seem to be tightening in Burundi, Nigeria, Russia, and Uganda. Currently an anti homosexual bill has been tabled in the Ugandan parliament. In December 2010, Member of Parliament, David Bahati, who authored the Bill told the Rachel Maddow Show that human rights do not apply to gays. The Bill proposes the arrest of people who engage in homosexual activity. The Bill also proposes execution for serial offenders.

Now I'd like to share what it was like for me to grow up in a severely homophobic familial and cultural environment in Jamaica.

CHAPTER 2

LEARNING TO FEAR, YET MAKING PROGRESS

I started Chapter 1 by recalling the shock of hearing my father, whom I loved dearly, advocating the killing of "those men." At the time, I was also frightened and confused. I was confused because the father I knew was not a violent man. He was a pillar of the Anglican Church. In fact he was a lay preacher. My siblings and I were brought up in the church. By the time I was in my teens, I was a Sunday school teacher. My understanding was that we were a God-fearing family. How, then, could my father be advocating violence? It was years before I understood that my father was **homophobic** and that in my beautiful Jamaica, verbal and physical violence against people who were gay or lesbian, or were assumed to be gay or lesbian, was not unusual. It was also years before I learned that many religious people base their antipathy to gays and lesbians on their interpretation of the Bible.

I am struck by how difficult it has been for me to remember anything else about my socialization regarding sexual identity. As a child, I do recall that from time to time a Rastafarian[1] with dreadlocks,[2] wearing ragged, filthy clothes, would come walking down the street yelling "sodomite" at odd intervals. He sounded fierce and angry, and I was terrified at the sight of him. Much later in life I discovered that "sodomite" was a crude reference to gay sex.

I wonder if the fact that I went to an Anglican girls' school from the age of ten to the age of eighteen, when I graduated, resulted in my limited knowledge of the pejorative terms that many kids learned early in life. Nevertheless, in that prim and proper environment, my friends and I giggled about our physical education teacher, who we thought looked and sounded like a man. Although we liked her very much and enjoyed her classes, that did not stop us from making fun of her—behind her back. We definitely thought that she was odd and strange. We weren't aware of the complexities of gender identity (congruence or incongruence between one's internal definition of self and one's biological sex). We also had never heard the term "gender expression," which refers to characteristics and behaviors that are defined by the dominant heterosexual group as feminine or masculine. But at that early age, we already sensed that there might be something "wrong" with her because she didn't fit our image of what a woman should look like. We also knew instinctively, it seemed, that it was not okay for a woman to have male characteristics. I do not remember a direct statement from any adult in my life that could have led me to such a conclusion. It seems that I absorbed ideas about what constituted "a real man" or "a real woman" from the atmosphere in which I grew up.

Many people, in my company workshops however, recall hearing the words "faggot," "sissy," "fairy," and "queer" hurled like missiles at kids who seemed in any way different on the playground. I do recall the pejorative term "batty man." As an adult I learned that this was the most derogatory description of a gay man that a Jamaican could make. "Batty man" was a vulgar reference to gay sex.

I also don't recall any conversations about heterosexuality. It seems that we took it for granted that people were heterosexual. I did figure out that since homosexuality was a "sin," God must have approved of people like us who were heterosexual. Homosexuals, on the other hand, were "moral degenerates" who had their being outside of the blessings of God.

My personal experience reflects what I've heard in workshops with hundreds of people over the years, across America and around the world. The majority of participants are able to recall from childhood negative things about gays and lesbians, and have little or no information to report about heterosexuals. In effect, heterosexuality was "normal," so there was no need to talk about it. This is similar to the way in which whites often know little about being white while having a lot of negative information about people of color. Indeed, in discussions about race, many have said, *"I never thought of myself as white before, and it feels really weird to think about it."*

This is the dominant/subordinated paradigm at work. Dominant group members typically focus more on "what is wrong" with subordinated group members while staying oblivious to the impact on subordinated group members of the prejudice and discrimination caused by their own group. Conversely, gays and lesbians as a subordinate group know a lot about heterosexuals. Their well being, and in some instances their lives, depends on it.

Is it any wonder, then, that writing about the oppression of gay, lesbian, and bisexual people is somewhat challenging for me as a heterosexual? Like concerned members of any dominant identity group, I fear that my own ignorance or unexamined prejudices and homophobia might emerge and cause offense, even when it is not intended. I grew up in a homophobic culture, so not surprisingly my learning curve has been steep.

In general, the world that we heterosexuals have created is homophobic. Despite some progress, the United States culture is homophobic. Here are some appalling statistics of violence against LGBT people in the United States:

> The total number of victims reporting anti-LGBT violence to the National Coalition of Anti-Violence Programs in 2008 was 2,424, which represents a 2 percent increase over the total number of victims reported in 2007 and a 26 percent increase over a two-year period. Known anti-LGBT murders rose 28 percent from 2007 to 2008 and are at the highest level since 1999.[3]

The statistics paint a bleak and sobering picture. Nevertheless, there are some hopeful signs in the United States. There is some public acknowledgement that there is a sexual orientation called heterosexuality and that it is not the only sexual orientation that exists. Regrettably, there is no such public acknowledgment in Jamaica, or in the Caribbean where constructive conversations about sexual orientation are rare. There is also no discernible support in either the private or public sectors for ending discrimination and violence against LGBT people.

The Human Rights Campaign (HRC) is the premier organization in the United States devoted to the achievement of civil rights and equality for the gay, lesbian, bisexual, and transgender population. The HRC states, *"Currently federal law provides basic legal protection against employment discrimination on the basis of race, gender, religion, national origin, or disability."*

So it is shocking that in the twenty-first century, there is still no federal anti-discrimination law that protects people who are lesbian, gay, bisexual or transgender. However, three states and the District of Columbia are leading the way. Nondiscrimination laws in Connecticut and Colorado protect against discrimination based on sexual orientation and gender identity. Delaware's nondiscrimination law protects against discrimination based on sexual orientation but not on gender identity. In 2009, President Obama signed into law the Matthew Shepard and James Byrd, Jr. Hate Crimes Prevention Act. Shepard was a white college student who was tortured and murdered because he was gay. James Byrd, Jr. was murdered because he was black. After the signing, the president observed, *"After more than a decade of opposition and delay, we've passed inclusive hate crimes legislation to help protect our citizens from violence based on what they look like, who they love, how they pray, or who they are."*[4]

Andrew Kessinger noted in an op-ed article in the *Washington Post*, *"Adding insult to injury, the measure had to be attached to a defense spending bill just to pass."*[5] So the forces for change in the United States have had to struggle long and hard for every inch of progress that has been made, and the forces that resist change continue to be powerful.

A number of corporations, including IBM, Lucent Technologies, Wachovia Bank, and Goldman Sachs, include heterosexism with their work on sexism and racism. Issues of bias and discrimination are discussed in workshops and in diversity councils. Some companies support employee networks for gay and lesbian employees, and some have extended domestic partner benefits to their lesbian and gay employees. Barney Frank is an openly gay congressman. Such a thing would be unthinkable in Jamaica. Although progress towards equality and justice for our LGBT population in the United States has been painfully slow, there is movement in the right direction. In my home of origin, the status quo remains intact.

In 2005, a prominent Jamaican politician made headlines with a public statement about his support for ongoing discrimination against lesbians and gays. In 2008, Jamaican Prime Minister Bruce Golding said he would not be pressured by outsiders to recognize homosexual rights. The prime minister was responding to a question on the BBC's *Hard Talk*. He went on to say, *"Sure, they can be in the Cabinet—but not mine!"*[6] Prime Minister Golding has also referred to gay advocates as *"perhaps the most organized lobby in the world."* He seemed to be suggesting that the struggle for equal rights was somehow sinister. The prime minister then said, *"We are not going to yield to the pressure, whether that pressure comes from foreign governments or groups of countries to liberalize the laws as it relates to buggery."*[7]

It is fair to say that the prime minister reflects the views of elements within both major political parties and the views of the Jamaican public overall. *Essence* magazine, in an in-depth article on homophobia in Jamaica, stated:

> The island's gay rights organization, Jamaica's Forum for Lesbians, All Sexuals, and Gays (J-Flag) notes that between 2006 and 2008 more than 150 homophobic assaults and murders were reported to the agency. Gay men and lesbians have been chased, chopped, beaten, raped and shot. But despite the gruesome nature of the attacks, many Jamaicans, including those in politics and law enforcement, insist that the situation is simply not as bad as the activists and foreign media make out.[8]

It is instructive to note that Jamaica is a small island with a population of approximately 2.7 million.

In the United States, bisexuals, gays, and lesbians are visible in the media, on television sitcoms as well as on talk shows. Increasingly, black as well as white leaders are vocal about the need to end discrimination based on sexual orientation and the importance of accepting gay, lesbian, and bisexual identity as part of the norm of the human family. We have a long way to go in the United States, but Jamaica is not even close to the level of public debate or private tolerance and acceptance that I see in the United States.

So, Jamaican children continue to learn about sexual identity from an intensely homophobic culture. In the United States, on the other hand, it appears that young people are increasingly supporting equal rights for gays and lesbians.

I have been concerned about the oppression of racism and sexism for most of my adult life. However, I turned a blind eye to the oppression of gays, lesbians, and bisexuals until my fourteen-year-old son confronted me. I was forty-one years old at the time. He had overheard his dad and me laughing at a so-called 'gay joke.' He looked us in the eye and asked, *"Would you really be laughing if there was someone gay in this room? Do you really think this is funny?"* He looked at us long and hard before striding out of the room. I was mortified. Can you imagine what it is like to be upbraided by your own teenage son? I turned to my husband and said, *"Douglas is right. This is not funny, is it? We've got to stop behaving like this."* To my enormous relief, he agreed. That was twenty-nine years ago. We made a commitment then to monitor our own prejudices and biases regarding gays, lesbians, and bisexuals. We've been intentional about building our awareness. And the reality is we still have a long way to go.

CHAPTER 3

DIALOGUE: BUILDING UNDERSTANDING AND CONNECTION

You are now about to read a transcript of a dialogue about sexual orientation that I had with a gay African American colleague, the Rev. Dr. Jamie Washington. Jamie is the president and founder of the Washington Consulting Group, a multicultural organizational development firm in Baltimore, Maryland. He is also a senior consultant with the Equity Consulting Group of California; with Elsie Y. Cross Associates of Philadelphia, the premier consulting firm on issues of diversity and inclusion; and with the Chambers Group Inc., a coaching firm in Charlotte, North Carolina. He has served as an instructor and educator in higher education for over twenty years. Most recently he was assistant vice president for student affairs at the University of Maryland Baltimore County (UMBC).

Jamie and I met a few years ago at a conference organized by the Chambers Group Inc. We also know each other indirectly through our membership in the professional network of Elsie Y. Cross Associates, Inc. Our dialogue about sexual orientation is based on a model called **"Dialogue with Difference: Skills for Managing Diversity."** Our colleague Delyte Frost, Ph.D., developed this model in 1984, and she revised it in 1996. Dr. Frost, who is a seasoned organizational development consultant, emphasizes that:

> to understand someone different than me requires that I move across a line or boundary that defines the difference. Issues of diversity—race, racism, gender, sexism, sexual orientation, heterosexism, culture, class, age, religious beliefs, abilities, and others—are complex, multifaceted, and carry with them the dynamic of dominant and subordinated group membership.

In the societal construct of dominance and subordination, dominant group members are accorded status, privilege, and acceptance because of a particular identity. Subordinated group members, on the other hand, are denied status, privilege, and acceptance because of their identity. Essentially, dominant groups are perceived to be superior, while subordinated groups are perceived to be inferior. The "Dialogue with Difference" model directs us to focus as dominant and subordinated group members on the different life experiences we have as a result of a particular social identity. Dominant group members learn about the reality of subordinated group members as they dialogue. Therefore, my dialogue with Jamie is about our different life experiences as a result of our sexual orientations. I am heterosexual, and therefore the dominant group member in our dialogue. Jamie is gay, and the subordinated group member in our dialogue. In the context of this model, Jamie has the opportunity and the authority to decide the focus of our dialogue. He has the power to direct the dialogue. This arrangement is contrary to the norm in society, where dominant group members typically, and unconsciously, take charge of the content and direction of conversations that they have with subordinated group members.

Jamie's openness to sharing his personal experience as a gay man, and the patterns of experience of gays, lesbians and bisexuals as a group, will be largely dependent on my willingness as a dominant group member to listen and hear, without judgment, what he has to say. My willingness to suspend my assumptions about the lesbian/gay/bisexual community will also affect the quality of our dialogue. Further, as our dialogue develops, Jamie will be able to figure out whether I am sincerely interested in learning about his reality based on my responses to him, my questions, my body language, as well as our previous limited history. What he may have heard about me from people he trusts may also play a part in the quality and honesty of our dialogue.

Our dialogue was unrehearsed. It was videotaped, and is recorded here with minor editing for clarity. Here is the transcript.

OUR DIALOGUE ABOUT SEXUAL ORIENTATION

SHIRLEY: Jamie, I can't tell you how happy I am that you are willing to have this dialogue with me and to take the time to be here. For me it's not only about business, but it's also an opportunity to get to know you. So thank you very much.

JAMIE: You are welcome. It's my pleasure to be here with you in your home...

SHIRLEY: I hope this will be the first of many visits. I want to start by asking a very broad question: what is life like for you as a gay man? I'll leave you to decide what direction you will take this.

JAMIE: As a gay man in the first decade of the twenty-first century—as a black gay man—there is so much intersection between race and sexual orientation—I don't think it's accidental that I am having this conversation with you today. I drove down here having a conversation with another black gay friend of mine about what life is like for us. We talked about the separation in our community. This separation is linked to religion, to HIV, to AIDS, and also to family. We talked about relationships. There is this added level of challenge as I think about what it is like particularly for men in relationships with other men. We are carrying around all of this stuff about sex stereotypes and what it means to be a man. What meaning do we make of gender expression or gender identity? What does it mean to be named as effeminate? All of that is playing out. So my relationship with a man is often challenging, with lots of bumps.

SHIRLEY: Does it get confusing at times?

JAMIE: It does get confusing, because the dynamic with men is that our socialization does not enable us to have conversation. This may not be so for all men, but most men don't know how to have conversations.

SHIRLEY: So gender gets in your way...

JAMIE: And gender gets in our way, so we are feeling all of this stuff, and we don't know how to talk about feelings, and we are not supposed to have feelings. Can I be a man and have feelings? Just all of that stuff! The result is, most of us show up in relationships often with very poor communication skills. Unless we are with someone else who understands these dynamics and is willing to engage, to put up with and deal, and see what's not being said and still give grace, it makes it difficult for relationships that are centered and loving. This is particularly true for black men. Again, I can't take out the race dynamics. As black men we deal with a lot every day; the racism, the way we are perceived, the disappointments, the expectations, the family, and all of that. I was talking with a friend of mine a week or so ago about an incident that occurred at one of the prominent churches in Washington, D.C. One of the ministers, I don't know if you heard about it, preached a really hateful, homophobic sermon. He called for the real men of the church to stand and come forward—no punks or faggots or sissies…

SHIRLEY: I did hear about it…was he an African American pastor?

JAMIE: He called for the "real men"—yes, this was an African American bishop, and he was one of my professors in seminary, so I know him well.

SHIRLEY: Oh my goodness…

JAMIE: He has a number of gay men in his congregation. Some gay friends of mine were at church that day. My friend asked them how they dealt with it and said that he was sure that they stayed in their seats in protest. They all said that they stood up, and walked to the front to be identified as "real men," not as faggots, punks, or sissies. If I had been there, I may have done the same thing, but I would have named the fact that I was walking forward as a whole, gay, real man. In the conversation with them, they said they could not bear the shame. They couldn't bear being identified as gay. They didn't want anyone to know that they are gay…as if nobody knows…

SHIRLEY: So he shamed them…

JAMIE: He shamed them. When I think about what it's like particularly for gay black men today, particularly after this heterosexism workshop that I just did, gender is a big deal for us. Who can we be? What is seen as okay? How do we share what's real for us as we try to deal with our internalized sexism and dominance as men? We want to be able to be all right, to be seen as just fully human with all the human feelings and emotions. Most of us men haven't developed the skills to be able to talk about what that is. We simply can't. There's a woman who talks about posttraumatic slave syndrome. Her name is...I'm blocking. She talks about the residual impact of slavery and what that means for us today. We are all living with it. What I got clear about is that many people in the gay community are living with posttraumatic AIDS syndrome, and it's not being talked about.

SHIRLEY: Even in the gay community?

JAMIE: Even in the gay community. So many folks have died, in such a short period of time and so quickly. The breadth and depth of talent that was lost. The pain of families and friends and the denial has been so intense. The way folks died and the way they were treated, we talk about it as a recent holocaust.

SHIRLEY: That's what it was...

JAMIE: It's just tragic, and the denial and the silence has led to the present face of AIDS in the black gay community with 48 percent of African American men living with HIV.

SHIRLEY: Forty-eight percent?

JAMIE: Forty-eight percent who are same-gender-loving African American men—that's almost every other man in our community. This is up for me right now because I took a friend of mine to the hospital last night. He discovered that he has full-blown AIDS. He would not get tested. He just lived in denial and in fear.

SHIRLEY: That sounds like an example of the posttraumatic stress. I can understand that suffering and death that is so vast and so intense could leave you frozen and really incapacitated, and unable to take care of yourself. It's too much to absorb and deal with. Someone I knew from my days at the University of the West Indies was in the diplomatic service here in the United States and was one of the first to die of AIDS. Initially no one knew what his illness was. It took the doctors a while to figure out that he in fact had AIDS. Before you could look around, he was gone. To have that multiplied by dozens and dozens of people, I can understand that an individual gay man could be so overwhelmed that he would freeze.

JAMIE: His family is in the West Indies. He said we shouldn't call his mom, so the community had to take care of him, or not take care of him. So gay men who become ill either have friends that will step up or step in and be with them, not just psychologically and emotionally, but also be there physically. "When I can't get up, can't get to the hospital, who is going to call my office?" So if you don't have a circle of friends who you can trust to do that for you and are able to because they have that flexibility in their own lives…

SHIRLEY: And the resources…

JAMIE: And have the resources, then you end up alone.

SHIRLEY: So it's like really needing to create a substitute family because your own family has not accepted that you are gay. And this is happening at a moment in your life when you don't have the time or the energy to manage the crisis you are in. In this particular case, is it that the family does not accept him as gay?

JAMIE: See, I don't even know if the family knows he's gay, and that's often the case in these last twenty years. More than a million people in the United States are infected with HIV. Nearly half of all people living with HIV in the United States are African American! (Note: the Centers for Disease Control report on estimated HIV incidence by race/ethnicity in 2006: blacks, 45 percent; whites, 35 percent; Hispanic/Latino, 17percent; Asian Pacific Islander, 2 percent; Native American, 1 percent.) We are talking about staggering numbers in the African American community. Living with HIV today is like living with diabetes. If you can take care of yourself, it's not a...

SHIRLEY: It's not a death sentence as it used to be.

JAMIE: No, it's not the death sentence that it used to be. But if it's not taken care of, it will be.

SHIRLEY: Part of what I'm thinking is how expensive these medicines are. How many people can afford these medicines? And are they widely available?

JAMIE: It's very expensive unless you can get into a program. Then you've got to make sure the medicines work with your system. The whole piece of it is pretty overwhelming. Right now I am particularly concerned for black men in our community who are living with this cloud and never really feeling safe or free. The threat is always there. We are always having the conversation about, or not having the conversation about, AIDS... If you've got hovering over you that this is God's punishment... if you are carrying any of that at any level, then it colors the way you show up in the world. So whether you are living with HIV, whether you have full-blown AIDS or not, if you are carrying that message...the number of blacks living with HIV is huge. Black men are six times more likely than are white men to get infected, and if they don't have the virus, well, look out, because it is God's punishment of gay men. It's the unspoken terror that manifests in alcohol abuse, drug abuse, sex abuse, addictions, and workaholism and religiosity/spiritual abuse. Folks will self-medicate with all of these things so as not to have to deal with the terror.

SHIRLEY: The thing that strikes me overwhelmingly as I listen to you is how unaware I have allowed myself to be, how unaware my group, heterosexuals, and in particular black heterosexuals have allowed ourselves to be. Somewhere in the back of my head, obviously I know that the incidence of AIDS in the black community is very high, and that it is growing. I believe there is a statistic that black women are contracting AIDS at a rate faster than any other group in the society. What I did not know is that the numbers of black men are as high as you just told me. So what hits me is that black men are in serious trouble. You notice that I am not saying black gay men, but black men, because that percentage of gay men with HIV is so high that that's also a huge percentage of black men overall, and so the question in me is, who cares?

JAMIE: Yes, who cares?

SHIRLEY: This is just stunning.

JAMIE: As you talk about the impact and the connection—men who have sex with other men includes men who are gay identified; some of them are bisexual identified; some of them are married; and so on and so forth. If you can't tell the truth, you are going home and having unprotected sex.

SHIRLEY: How do you say to your wife, "we need to use condoms?"

JAMIE: What gets blamed is the gay community. Gay people get blamed, not heterosexism or homophobia. It's not the system that allows that to stay in place that is blamed. Married men shouldn't be out cheating, and we also know that the virus is transferred not only by sex. If I'm exchanging needles and then have sex then I could still be exchanging the fluids. The numbers overall are devastating for the black community.

SHIRLEY: And for the society... As black heterosexuals, we place the blame on individual black men. That allows us to avoid examining the role of the black community as a whole, or the role of society. That way we don't have to try to figure out what we need to do systemically to try and change this situation. The other thing that strikes me, too, and I don't know that I've thought about it in quite this way before, but black gay men are on their own in terms of trying to figure out this mess.

JAMIE: That's right.

SHIRLEY: There isn't much the society is providing by way of resources, and the homophobia of my group makes it very difficult to reach out to even have the conversation.

JAMIE: Exactly. I'm just thinking about the fact that the first face of AIDS was white gay men. That's what it was. It was the racism that had us be delusional.

SHIRLEY: Yes, I remember that this was a "white disease" up to the mid '80s. This had nothing to do with black people.

JAMIE: I actually knew black people who had died but didn't know why. "What happened to him?" Then we started hearing about AIDS, but the face was white because, who mattered? At the same time, blacks were dying at an alarming rate without resources and so forth. The other side to this is that currently there are great medicines. You can live healthy and you can live long. There are lots of folks who have been living with HIV for eighteen to twenty years. Some folks have been living with full-blown AIDS and are pretty healthy without frequent bouts of illness.

SHIRLEY: The medications are amazing.

JAMIE: There are lots of theories out there that there is a cure but it wouldn't be good for business to share that. There's also the theory that the virus of HIV does not cause AIDS. There are questions about how much of this is about keeping drug companies in business. People pay high prices for drugs to stay alive. So, it's this backdrop, this cloud but it doesn't have to be the definer of one's existence. But it is something that the black gay community cannot escape or the gay community as a whole cannot escape.

SHIRLEY: Or the society as a whole, even though we are trying so hard. The other thing that is hitting me as I listen to you is that this is a disease that impacts every area of the society. You've made linkages to race, socioeconomic class, religion, and gender. There are tentacles that are reaching into every part of who we are as people. And yet we continue to pretend that somehow this is a problem that we can marginalize. We don't have to pay full attention to it. It's pretty overwhelming.

JAMIE: So I have that as a backdrop, and then I have, particularly from the black community, religion as well. So much of the American black experience is related to religion. The Christian church also informs blacks raised in the Caribbean.

SHIRLEY: Oh! Absolutely. "Without my religion I would not have survived." That's like a theme throughout the black Diaspora in the Western world.

JAMIE: And the messages from that space, from religion, for the most part, have not been supportive of gay and lesbian existence. So there is an enormous amount of internalized oppression and self-hate that exists within the black gay community. I think it's deeper than just race, for at present racism is not reaffirmed in church every Sunday. There is a lot to counter the negative messages about being black, although there is all this negative stuff in the media. For example, blacks are criminals, but then you get to see a Cornel West, a Bill Cosby, and your mom...

SHIRLEY: You see the positive sides of being black.

JAMIE: And you don't go to church on Sunday and hear that because you're black, God doesn't love you and either you change or you...you make God sick...

SHIRLEY: You've actually heard somebody say that?

JAMIE: Oh! Absolutely, absolutely. Because you are gay, you make God vomit. With that level of hatred coming at you…I tell folks all the time you don't have to go to church to be impacted negatively by religion, especially in the black community. Lots of black gays don't go to church, but their mother or aunt does, or their grandparent does. Sometimes the woman down the street is giving a mother Christian tracts for her gay child. All of these kinds of things happen, so the mother wonders if she should be supportive of her gay child. She might not feel like she is as holy as "sister girl" who hands out the tracts. She may feel that she isn't good at all because she was a teenage mom, and that the sister handing out tracts is more righteous than she is. She's got better relations with God. She really thinks homosexuality is wrong. She thinks, "Maybe I really shouldn't be supporting my child even though in my heart I want to…"

SHIRLEY: So people are being pulled in different directions…

JAMIE: Pulled and tugged in all kinds of ways. I often talk about my experience in seminary. I sat through seminary for three years of intensive studies for pastors-to-be. We were being trained to be the spiritual leaders, spiritual holders, for our communities. The last semester—Shirley, one thing I was determined about—I was not going to be in seminary and not be out as a gay man…

SHIRLEY: I was just going to ask you about that…

JAMIE: How can you be in seminary and not be out? God already knows you are gay, right? Well, I was very surprised that many folks were not out. At least four or five people in my class were not out at all. So about four others and me were the poster children. One of them was younger, one was white, and so they wrote him off. This was Howard University, a black seminary. But I was the thorn in their flesh because I'm black. I looked like the professors, and I looked like their pastors. "He sounds like one of us, and when he talks, his spirit is like ours. What does he mean that he is gay and that God intended that?" So I went to seminary, and I knew that I was going to be out and that I was not going to do a whole lot of talking about being gay. I was not going to be doing a lot of papers on being gay, but then God said, "Oh yes you are. Because that's exactly why I sent you here." We had Christian Social Ethics, Biblical Studies papers and presentations, and as soon as the topic came around, I knew that I would have to be the one to talk about homosexuality. I found myself doing presentations, and my fellow students would ask questions: "How do I go back and deal with this issue? What am I supposed to say to my congregation?"

SHIRLEY: So you were in effect educating your class and your faculty…

JAMIE: Exactly. We are studying the same Bible and we all know as we are studying that those texts and scriptures that have been historically used to condemn gays, lesbians, and bisexual folks have been misused. They have been misinterpreted. Anyone who is a real scholar reviewing the original text would say that this is simply a matter of interpretation that has resulted in heterosexism and homophobia. The Bible was never meant to be a science book. It was pre-science, and we know more about sexuality and sexual orientation today than was known when the Bible was written. So we are all sitting there reading this, learning this. So what do you mean, what are you going to go back to your parishioners and say? You have to tell the truth. Right?

"OHHH—how can I go back and say that?" We got to the last semester and I realized that we only had three weeks left, and there were some important issues that we needed to talk about. We had a senior seminar focused on discussion, and our professor thought it was a great idea to deal with unfinished business. We've been in seminary for three years. Now we were going out with the official credentials to lead congregations, to pastor, in any denomination we might choose..."

SHIRLEY: What a responsibility...

JAMIE: What's the unfinished business? The professor sent out an e-mail asking us to come prepared to talk about unfinished business and to have authentic dialogue. So we get to class, walk into the room, and the professor asks, "What's unfinished?" (Jamie looks around rolling his eyes).

SHIRLEY: Nobody speaks!

JAMIE: Right, nobody is saying anything! I look at my classmates wondering if they have four heads or something...

SHIRLEY: And these are all men?

JAMIE: No, there were men and women. Actually there are about 60 percent men and 40 percent women today in seminary at Howard. That's been the shift in terms of gender and religion. There are now women pastors. This is a major shift that the church has been dealing with. And, lots of these women pastors are still in churches where they have not been ordained as reverends.

SHIRLEY: But they are trained pastors...

JAMIE: Exactly, and they are staying. But anyway, back to the seminar. Nobody had anything to say. I said, "I got some unfinished business. Let's talk about sexuality, period. Let's talk about how we are dealing with sexuality in the church." I'm not just talking about how it relates to sexual orientation for gays, lesbians, and bisexuals.

SHIRLEY: You were talking broadly about sexual behavior...

JAMIE: Yes, about sexuality, period. What are we saying to the fifty-year-old or forty-five-year-old widow who has no intention of marrying again? Is her sex life over? Is she going to be living in sin if she develops a sexual relationship? Is that what we are telling her? What's the message that we are giving to the senior couple who have found each other in their autumn years? They may be sixty-five or seventy years old and their partners have transitioned, or they were never partnered. If they marry, that may negatively impact their Social Security. If they proceed as partners, are they living in sin? Can they have sex? They are not officially married...

SHIRLEY: Also, what are pastors saying to young people?

JAMIE: There is so much that we need to say about sexuality. It's not only about sexual orientation. Young people come home talking about what they feel about what's going on inside of their own bodies. For example: my best friend is gay, or my friend is lesbian, and why is it that they are not okay? How are we teaching parents and young people in our churches to have this conversation? I went through all of that, and I talked about a whole bunch of other stuff—heaven and hell and death, I just listed all these things. So we are having this good conversation. One colleague jumps up and says, "We had it at my church."

SHIRLEY: Had what?

JAMIE: What is the "it" that we are talking about? The "it" was homosexuality. The class ended and three people in that class who had been with me for three years came to me afterwards. Two of them have lesbian daughters. A woman colleague told me that her husband is gay and the father of a child. None of them knows how to deal with it. All of them were in deep struggle, trying to engage and think about how to navigate and talk about this complexity. What is God's real intention and what is his will for us? For three years, nobody said a word. I think the impact that the black church has, whether people are part of it or not, is very real. So if people are disconnected from the church, what that means for lots of folks is disconnection from their spirituality, because they have not found any other way to access Spirit. So even if they have done other things that are spiritually fulfilling, they have not coded it as that. So they live amorphous lives, and when something goes awry that they can't explain…

SHIRLEY AND JAMIE: They have nowhere to turn.

JAMIE: Everywhere I go, and I travel all over the country, as I talk about the experience of black lesbians, and gay people, the impact of religion is always in the room.

SHIRLEY: Absolutely.

JAMIE: And those who are not members of the church feel marginalized because they are not members. They may say, "I didn't grow up in the black church, so I can't fully understand how anybody could sit in a church like the one where there was this hateful sermon (that I talked about)—how could anybody do that?" When something hateful like that is said to somebody who is a part of the church, then they are not only disconnected from the church, they are disconnected from the black community as well. And it's not just the gay people who can sit there in the face of such bigotry, it's also the heterosexuals who will sit there and allow that...

SHIRLEY: Yes.

JAMIE: It's family members of gays as well who remain silent. How could people just allow ministers to get away with that?

SHIRLEY: It seems to me that you are also saying that there is a huge leadership role that the black church needs to play. Traditionally the church has always played a significant leadership role in the black community. It sounds as if what you are saying is that the leaders of the black church are failing in that responsibility.

JAMIE: That's right.

SHIRLEY: If you can't have these conversations about sexuality in seminary, where can you have them? By the way, when were you in seminary?

JAMIE: I just finished in 2004.

SHIRLEY: This is incredible. You are not describing a situation that existed forty years ago; you are talking about current times.

Turning out pastors who are not equipped to have these conversations with members of their congregations is a very scary proposition.

JAMIE: Absolutely.

SHIRLEY: I saw recently that Reverend Al Sharpton, American Baptist minister, civil rights activist, and radio talk show host, is speaking out clearly on these issues. I was just so relieved to hear that, because I don't know of many religious leaders in the black community who are being that open on the subject of sexual orientation.

JAMIE: And are identified as heterosexual? Many in our society write Al (Sharpton) off as crazy. E. Michael Dyson, the Rev. Dr. Michael Dyson, American academic, author, professor of sociology at Georgetown University, calls us to task on this issue all the time. Cornel West, the Rev. Dr. Cornel West, as well, academic, author, professor of religion and director of Afro-American studies at Princeton University.

SHIRLEY: Yes, yes, of course...

JAMIE: These are the academics, theologians, that many want to sideline because "they got so much intellect that they ain't got no Jesus."

SHIRLEY: Is that what people say about them? (Both Shirley and Jamie laugh out loud)

JAMIE: "They ain't got nothing to do with God. They are just catering to the world."

SHIRLEY: Or politically they are so left wing, so radical, that we cannot take them seriously?

JAMIE: That's right.

SHIRLEY: But thank God for them.

JAMIE: Exactly. Some of the religious leaders will try to write him off, but there are a lot of people who listen to Al Sharpton.

SHIRLEY: Well, yes, he is a very astute man.

JAMIE: Many people are very challenged by him.

SHIRLEY: Yes, I think that's because he is intellectually very competent.

JAMIE: That's right, so he challenges them. "Oh my goodness, did Al Sharpton say this?" He is a very powerful force. The National Black Justice Coalition, which is the national black gay and lesbian leadership organization, held a religious forum in Atlanta. Reverend Sharpton was their keynote speaker. There were a whole slew of religious leaders who made strong anti-gay statements, and these were black church leaders. Not only am I concerned about the impact of black clergy on black gay people in our community; I am particularly concerned about the impact on children. Do we think that black gay people spring forth full-grown?

SHIRLEY: Right. Sometimes I think that we heterosexuals act that way.

JAMIE: There are black gay and lesbian children sitting in churches...

SHIRLEY: Being vilified by their pastors...

JAMIE: This happens continuously, and so we are creating another generation of self-hating folks with low self-esteem.

SHIRLEY: So we are destroying ourselves.

JAMIE: We are destroying ourselves.

SHIRLEY: AIDS is one thing, but we are also doing it ourselves.

JAMIE: That's right.

SHIRLEY: I have great respect for Reverend Sharpton, because he dares to speak out on homophobia in our community. It's even more impressive because he is really marginalized politically, precisely because he speaks out so directly on the issues that are affecting our society. In Jamaica we have a saying about somebody who speaks out directly and honestly like that: "Him not talking with water in him mouth." That means you don't have to wonder where someone is on an issue. And as a result he is not only marginalized but, I think it's fair to say, demonized to a large degree by various political pundits. I think that because he is so competent intellectually, they don't know how to respond to him. No matter what you throw at him, Al will respond powerfully in a nanosecond.

JAMIE: So you can't just discount him.

SHIRLEY: No, you can't.

JAMIE: So you have to do something in your head with that dissonance...

SHIRLEY: And it's true, too, of Reverend Dyson.

JAMIE: Oh yes.

SHIRLEY: It's very interesting how little I see of him in the national media. I've seen him on Bill Maher's show and on PBS. He doesn't seem to get many opportunities to speak on the national stage.

JAMIE: That's right, because he calls folks to task on heterosexism and homophobia, and he talks about the plight of the black community. He is also a strong supporter of hip-hop culture.

SHIRLEY: He also speaks out on immigration and links the struggle for bisexual, gay, and lesbian rights to the civil rights movement in the '60s. I really do think that the society is not that interested in hearing from many of our powerful black leaders. At this point in our dialogue, Jamie, I want you to know that the fact that you started by talking about the devastation caused by HIV and AIDS in the black community had a powerful impact on me. I do appreciate your sharing with me as openly as you have, because it takes me to another level of understanding and insight about what is happening to black men, and to black gay men in particular. But speaking more generally, as you go around the country, do you feel safe? Do you have concerns about your safety as a gay black man? I hear you consistently making that linkage between sexual orientation, race, and gender, and I am seeing how hard it is to disentangle these identities.

JAMIE: I am buffered by social class, academics, gender identity, and expression privilege. I can also pass as a heterosexual. My size and how I express myself provide a buffer for me from a lot of prejudices that other members of my group experience.

SHIRLEY: So Dr. Jamie Washington gets a level of respect that your ordinary guy on the street does not get.

JAMIE: Yes, and when you add Reverend Doctor to that…

SHIRLEY: Reverend Doctor, yes, of course…

JAMIE: Many anti-gay folks will attack on the basis of religion. My training makes that approach difficult and challenging. That does not mean that safety is not an issue. Just yesterday I was talking with a friend about being held up at gunpoint when I was sixteen years old. I knew I was gay, and that God didn't want that, so I got delivered from homosexuality. I was just walking in my holy straightness, thank you, Lord. (Jamie laughs.) So I was walking down the street going to church. Some guys ran up to me at gunpoint and said, "We don't allow faggots down here. If you come back, we will kill you." I was confused. How could they still think that I was a faggot? After all, God had delivered me. That was major confusion for this sixteen-year-old child. God wasn't pleased with who I was, and I thought I'd done what I needed to do to change that. How could this be happening? And even if I were gay, why did I deserve to be killed? Literally for the next five years, I could not walk on that street. So I went the long way 'round to go to church out of fear. I didn't realize how much of that fear I still carried until I moved to Baltimore, and I lived off campus for the first time. Previously, I had lived in residence halls. When I moved to Baltimore and lived on my own for the first time, one of the guys I was dating was effeminate, was more stereotypically gay. People could tell. Some children started calling us names. These were nine- to ten-year-old children. I remember when I got out of my car at night, I would look around as I was going into my apartment, for fear that someone would try to do me harm. When I moved into my house I still carried that fear. There were days when my partner and I would find trash on our lawn, beer bottles, etc. Sometimes people harassed us. I wanted to have a dog out of fear that something bad might happen, that someone might become violent. So at some subconscious level, always back there in my mind is the knowledge that there are people who would do me harm. As I said, I am buffered because most folks don't know or can't tell that I'm gay. I don't live in an environment that is not safe, as far as any community is safe for gays. There is always this low-grade fear of physical violence, but there is also always the fear of loss. I live with the constant threat of loss.

SHIRLEY: And that loss could be of a heterosexual friend who discovers that you are gay; it could be loss in terms of AIDS literally taking somebody away?

JAMIE: Given the work that we both do, we make deep connections with people. When I walk into a conference room in corporate America, the subordinated group members are typically glad that I am there, or they hope they are going to be glad that I am there. (Both Jamie and Shirley laugh.)

SHIRLEY: That's right.

JAMIE: I just know black participants are thinking, "Let's hope this isn't an idiot they've brought in who is going to be toeing the party line." Then they see me naming issues of racism and it's "Hallelujah, thank you, God, I am not alone." Black people need me to show up black, i.e., be aware of the impact of racism. They are so grateful to see me, and when the religious ones discover that I am a reverend, they too are really happy.

SHIRLEY: So I am guessing that they feel that they love Jamie.

JAMIE: Yes, and they are grateful. And then they learn that other thing, that I am gay. And then, there is loss. What I often experience is loss on several levels. I lose black people, period, and often they don't seem to even realize that we have gone from deep connection, hanging out at breaks, etc., to complete disconnection.

SHIRLEY: Yes, that's when they've discovered that you are "one of them."

JAMIE: Yes, then the Christians, white and black, who were happy to hear me name myself as Christian almost seem to collapse when they discover that I am gay. "How can you say that you are a Christian and then say that you are gay?" So I lose the Christians. And the greatest loss for me is the loss of black men, because the experience of black men in our society is one like no other. This makes me think about issues of people who are transgender. When a female transitions to male in the society and that person is white, he goes up in status.

SHIRLEY: Oh, absolutely.

JAMIE: When it's a black transitioning from female to male, his status decreases. As I've talked with my transgender male friends, they tell me how painful it was for them to really see that there is a different level of prejudice that comes at black men. So, given that, the worst thing for a black man is to be without his brothers.

SHIRLEY: Because then you are truly isolated. Given that it is your typical experience in a diversity workshop that blacks desert you and that Christians desert you, do you have any experience of support, and where does it come from?

JAMIE: It comes from white women. That's where the support automatically comes from. I was not always conscious of this ongoing loss, neither was I aware of the impact it was having on me. It's always a challenge for me to decide when to "come out" as gay in a workshop. It is important to me to be authentic in these workshops, so I have to be "out" at some point. I finally started to say to participants: Here is what typically happens: Christians, you are all about to go away. Black people, black men, that connection we've had for the last three days? It's over." As a black gay man when I show up in the world, every week it is a constant loss. Sometimes I have the energy to deal with the loss, sometimes I don't. In those situations, I don't come "out." What I realize is that once I started naming this dynamic of loss, it stopped happening. I actually don't believe that people want to go away, to isolate me. I don't believe the Christians want to go away or that black people want to go away. So they go on automatic mode. I've had black men come up to me and say, "If you hadn't explained your sense of loss, I'd be gone."

SHIRLEY: Your naming that reality must have an enormous impact. I don't think that in the moment that people are even conscious that they are going away, deserting you, but when you name it for them, they have to confront it.

JAMIE: "We are black men. We don't deal with fags, but your naming your experience of loss, that makes me conscious." I think that that's what happens. At that point folks start talking about their cousins and other relatives who are gay, lesbian, or bisexual.

SHIRLEY: That must take a workshop to a whole other level. It has to.

JAMIE: They tell me that their cousins, brothers, their uncles have left the family; that they got sick and died; that Dad has never gotten over the fact that he didn't go to see his brother when he was sick. They have had no space to talk about these things. Heterosexism impacts all of us and our ability to relate to each other as members of the community. As black people, we don't typically throw each other away.

SHIRLEY: No, we don't. Something else just came to mind. I am remembering the statement you make to groups, "You are about to go away." I am guessing that you are saying it from a place of deep compassion, and that that is what enables people to move towards you versus move away from you. Am I right?

JAMIE: Yes, because I do understand…

SHIRLEY: So it's not a condemnation of people that you are making.

JAMIE: No, as I sit and listen, I believe their hearts would say no…

SHIRLEY: Any human heart, you would think.

JAMIE: That's right.

SHIRLEY: But the society, our homophobia, tells them something else.

JAMIE: Yes— "If I move towards Jamie, what will that mean? I have to protect myself and keep my distance. I have to protect not only my family, but also my image." This loss of brothers for me is so significant. What just clicked for me is the impact of J. L. King's book *On the Down Low*, which speaks about men who have intimate relationships with women and who also have sex with men. They don't say that they are gay. When Oprah had King on, back in '04, she asked him, "What are you?" He couldn't identify.

SHIRLEY: He could not name himself as gay.

JAMIE: He couldn't name himself. Where do we learn about sexual orientation? We aren't taught about sexuality, and the difference between sexual orientation and sexual behavior and gender identity…

SHIRLEY: In fact, King was saying that not only was he not gay, but that the men he knew who were on the down low were not gay either.

JAMIE: Why would he say that? What is his construction of "gay?" What does it mean that he would say that? It seems to me a lack of understanding about sexual orientation, and the complex nature of sexuality. I can understand why he would say it. However, that doesn't mean that he is not gay or possibly bisexual. It's just that given his understanding and knowledge about what sexual orientation is…

SHIRLEY: Equally, I can understand that Oprah and her audience would be totally confused.

JAMIE: Exactly—how could they not be confused?

SHIRLEY: Of course, Oprah has done a great job educating the public about prejudice and discrimination against people who are LGBT...

JAMIE: Exactly. But what do we know about gender identity, or gender expression?

SHIRLEY: It would be great to see our colleagues who have been working on issues of identity for years engaging the public in the media, on talk shows, etc. I'm sure you've heard J. L. King's statement that he is no longer on the "down low." In fact, he is a motivational speaker on issues of gender identity, HIV/AIDS, etc.

JAMIE: And that is wonderful. The impact of the DL (Down Low) on black men and our relationships has been enormous. As a black gay man, when I talk with my heterosexual black male friends, it has created a wedge. If they are single and feel comfortable with gay men, then they are questioned.

SHIRLEY: Absolutely, and then when they are with women, they are suspect.

JAMIE: That's right. A friend told me he was dating this woman for the first time and that he talked comfortably about heterosexism and homophobia with her. She was immediately suspicious and told him that he could be on the DL.

SHIRLEY: So another wedge...

JAMIE: So black men feel threatened. "How do I have a conversation about sexuality or sexual orientation? Can I be friends with Jamie?" It's guilt by association. "I've got to keep my distance from him." So we stay divided and disconnected. I keep looking at that painting on the wall. Is it a child?

SHIRLEY: Oh, that's a woman on the beach.

JAMIE: I keep thinking about the children. I think that's because of my nephew's graduation from St. Mary's College. He is a gay child who grew up with me in the church from the time he was eight, nine years old. He came out to me at age sixteen. When he came out, it was after we had a new pastor. For eight of those years, we served under a pastor who, while he was not gay affirming from the pulpit, he was not gay condemning either. That's the other key dynamic for black gay folks; we take what we can get.

SHIRLEY: I understand that.

JAMIE: We learn to settle. At least this pastor is not condemning me to hell...

SHIRLEY: So, therefore, he is a wonderful man?

JAMIE: Right. Or at least your family hasn't put you out. They don't accept your love. You can't bring him home, but they know you are gay.

SHIRLEY: But at least there is some tolerance and you are grateful for it.

JAMIE: That's right. We learn to live with less, to accept what we can get. I can't begin to talk about how that manifests in all the areas of our lives—work, relationships, family. We learn to take what we can get. But this child, my nephew, came out to me along with another gay child in the church who I didn't know. The pastor I told you about was gay affirming outside of the pulpit. He would say, for example, that God loves all people, and God can save gay people just like he saves everybody else. It was obvious that he knew I was gay. He loved me. He supported my partner and me. I was a leader in the church. So it was enough for me, because I had what I needed—a black church worship experience. If you are a black gay person and the church is a part of your identity and your worship experience, you want to stay a part of it, because the church is community for us. If you don't want to lose that you learn to settle. Some gay folks will settle for what happened at Mount Calvary, which would have been over the edge for me. Some gay folks would not support a pastor who could not affirm gays and who made heterosexist comments from the pulpit. The assumption of heterosexuality was okay with them. Anyway, this pastor left and we got a new pastor. Her mission was to eradicate homosexuality from the church. That's what she said her calling was.

SHIRLEY: She was explicit about it.

JAMIE: My nephew and this other child came out to me after she had been there for about five months. They said to me, "She is killing us. My friends tell me that after I've gone to church on Sunday that they don't see me again until Wednesday. They tell me that my body is there, but I am not there. That the spirit of life and energy and effervescence is not there."

SHIRLEY: So these children were going to church, were at worship, in a poisoned atmosphere. What does that do to somebody?

JAMIE: Children are being killed psychologically. Parents are being poisoned against their family members. It was the start of my clarity about what God needed me to do. I had previously spoken out about the church, and its role in homophobia and heterosexism, everywhere but in the church itself. I was out in the world consulting, keynoting, and training. I was talking about the church, but not in the church, or to the church. I got clear that I had to confront my abuser. So my calling is about reconciliation and healing, not only for gays and lesbians who have been disconnected from the church and from their divinity in God because of heterosexism and homophobia, but also for anybody else, because of what people have done in the name of God. And of course this abuse has nothing to do with God. My primary focus has been the impact on children, because that's when I first experienced abuse in the church. Typically when we talk about the language of abuse, we don't often talk about it in the context of religion and spirituality. In reality religion and spirituality are very powerful, insidious, abusive tools. People who self-medicate sometimes use religion as part of their self-medication.

SHIRLEY: I am also thinking, as I listen to you, about the many ways historically in which religion has been used to justify oppression. I've just returned from a vacation in Hawaii. It was only one hundred years ago that the people lost their country, and pretty much in the name of religion. It was Christian missionaries who paved the way for the conquest of Hawaii. They had to "save these heathens," bring them into the fold, and in the process take away their history, their land. Hawaiians are now a tiny minority of landowners in their own country. Their language is disappearing.

Their culture is disappearing. Religious oppression is a part of our reality, i.e., "My God is the one and only God. Your beliefs are different from mine, so you are outside of God's grace." I certainly share your concern about children. About ten years ago I found myself wondering, what if my grandchildren are gay, lesbian, bisexual, or transgender? I knew that I would continue to love them, and that I would do everything I could to protect them from homophobia and heterosexism. But the reality is, if they had been born twenty-five years ago, I don't know that I would have taken that position. I would have seen them as somehow outside of the blessing of God. As a Jamaican woman coming out of a severely homophobic culture, there is a part of me that says that if I could increase my awareness and become compassionate on this issue, others can, too. So a question that I have for you is, do you have any hope of substantive change on these issues, particularly in the black community?

JAMIE: See, I live in hope and faith in us as a people and in human beings in general. I couldn't do my social justice work without it. It's not Pollyanna hope. It is based on what I see. It is this conversation. This is real. I am having this conversation with a woman who I admire and respect, and who is my senior. You come from such a homophobic background and experience, yet you have grown and developed to the point that we can have this conversation. It will be recorded in a book that will be helpful and supportive to people. Being a part of a church ministry that is gay affirming, and being an associate pastor in a church where literally we bring together over a hundred people who are gay, lesbian, or transgender, as well as heterosexual allies, to worship, gives me hope.

SHIRLEY: That is amazing. Is this church Unity?

JAMIE: Yes, it's Unity Fellowship Church of Baltimore. There are fifteen of these churches across the country. Hope is being at the Unity Fellowship church midyear meeting in Arlington, Virginia. Nearly six hundred of us were there for service from around the country with the archbishop who is the founder of the movement. He founded the movement at the height of the AIDS crisis because churches were not administering funerals for their leaders—their choir directors, ministers of music, and ushers who were dying of AIDS.

SHIRLEY: That is chilling. They would not bury their dead.

JAMIE: They would not bury their dead. The movement was founded so that the trauma that was occurring could be managed. This was a situation where we were going to funerals every week at that time in the mid to late '80s. It was that intense.

SHIRLEY: So, was this church founded by a black...?

JAMIE: Our founder is an African American gay man who had once attempted suicide, because it wasn't okay for him to be gay. He founded the movement. On his bed in the hospital as they were reviving him from his attempted suicide, the nurse said, "God's got something for you to do." He said yes to the Lord at that point and started the church. He's from Baltimore. He was a singer and theater performer. He started the church in his home in 1980. Twenty-five years later there are fifteen churches and we are growing. So as I talk about being hopeful, Unity Fellowship is the largest official black gay-affirming movement. There are other churches that are black and gay affirming. We try to connect with all of those. There are probably another thirty or so around the country. And there are others that are "don't ask, don't tell." The ministers know there are gays in the congregation, and it's a supportive environment, but "we don't talk a lot about it." And then there are heterosexual leaders like Reverend Al Sharpton, and the Reverend Dyson and Cornel West, and there are pastors like Jeremiah Wright, pastor emeritus of the Trinity United Church of Christ in Chicago, and Peter Gomes American Baptist Minister and theologian at Harvard University Divinity School, who are speaking out on issues of discrimination in the gay/lesbian community. All of this gives me hope. I am not surprised that homophobia comes out of the mouths of religious leaders. I don't, however, expect it as much from professors in seminary. Even if they are homophobic, I expect them to couch it. But there was a professor who didn't in a class one day. There were only a few of us who spoke up on the issues, i.e., two friends and me, one of whom was white. We were there in the class. The professor started talking about one of his parishioners who lived in a rented space belonging to the church. The professor's wife found a gay video in this apartment, and she called her husband and told him he had to come and see this immediately.

SHIRLEY: This was a huge calamity.

JAMIE: Oh! He said he saw the worst thing that he could ever have seen in his life. He went on and on with the most hateful homophobic stuff. I was sitting there stunned. The three of us looked at each other. Who would say something? Others in the class started to join the professor. Then my white friend, Jim, with all his white entitlement, jumped in to the conversation. He said, "Hell no, you all think I'm crazy anyway, because I am the only white student at this black seminary." He confronted the professor, and then I jumped in to support him. The following year we were in another class with the same professor, and one of the students started talking in a homophobic way, and to my amazement, the professor said, "You just keep praying. I was right where you were. I am sixty-five years old, and I'm not finished. You are not finished yet either."

SHIRLEY: That's a great story.

JAMIE: Yes, when we show up authentically, we create the space for others to learn, to confront their own stuff.

SHIRLEY: And we create the space for others to speak. Jim spoke up and your professor heard him. He was able to learn and grow from the experience. That gives me hope ,too. If I didn't believe that human beings were capable of change, I could not do the work that I am doing either. It's hard to deal with the anger, fear, and hostility in the society in general on issues relating to sexual orientation and transgender. However, I recognize the potential for some positive outcomes. On the surface it looks and sounds horrible, but once this ugliness starts to be expressed, people react. Many are shocked and dismayed at the level of hate. That then allows for the possibility of change, of movement in a direction towards our common humanity. We know ourselves to be human, and we allow others to be just as human as we are.

JAMIE: Yes, absolutely. I also find joy in my own family. I have four nephews. I am the only male child born in my generation. I am the primary male figure in their lives. They respect and adore me. They treat me and my partner like gold. We laugh, we play, and we talk about relationships. One is thirty; one twenty-three and just had a baby; another is nineteen, and one is sixteen. The two youngest have called my partner "Uncle" since they were children. Especially for black men, this is precious. I don't know how they deal with the topic of sexual orientation when I'm not around, but they bring all their friends to their home when I'm there.

SHIRLEY: You're like a father figure to them.

JAMIE: Exactly. My nephews are all partnered with women at this point. They are delightful. So my family is a wonderful place of hope. I wouldn't want to end my conversation without saying that I count it all joy to have had the life experience that I have. There have been some bumps and some struggles. However, some of my deepest friendships and connections have been as a result of being a black gay male. I understand, I connect with and have met people and gone places that I never would have gone otherwise. As I think about community, some of my most fun times are on Sunday morning when I'm with that black gay congregation and our heterosexual allies. Kathy and Paulette's wedding in Massachusetts, with all just wonderful allies, all being human and loving... (Kathy and Paulette are lesbian colleagues.)

SHIRLEY: I told Kathy and Paulette that I've never experienced a wedding with such an overflow of love. It was an amazing experience.

JAMIE: Absolutely. I remember it was 1992 when I stood up at a national black gay and lesbian conference in a worship service, and I said publicly for the first time that I thank God for the gift of my homosexuality. As I said it, people looked at me and saw this as a revolutionary statement. But I understood that this is not a curse, and that I celebrate being created just as I am, and I'm so grateful for it. I have had all this joy and laughter and struggles, but 90 percent of the time I love life and everything that comes with it. A key part of that is about being black and gay. We are connected to family. I would not want anything different. I wish the level of love and respect and connection that I have for myself and from others, for everybody. Paulette and Kathy sent flowers to my mother on Mother's Day. They met my mom at my graduation from seminary and they just fell in love with her. I could hear in my mother's voice her appreciation, how much it meant to her that these white women from New England would honor her in that way. I wish that level of connection and community and love for everybody. It comes from a deep level of compassion and understanding of what the pain of oppression can do.

SHIRLEY: Absolutely. I think that this is a wonderful moment to put a comma in our conversation. Thank you, Jamie; you are so precious. Now that you are in my life, I hope you know that you are in my life. (Shirley and Jamie hug.) I can't imagine it without you now.

JAMIE: Thank you for that. It's been such a gift to have this conversation with you. Just wonderful…Just wonderful…

CHAPTER 4

CLOSING REFLECTIONS

At the start of my first chapter, I described the challenging journey that has finally led me to accept the full humanity of gay, lesbian, and bisexual people. It is painful for me to acknowledge that my advocacy and concerns about social justice for women, and for people of color, precluded any consideration whatsoever about the plight of people who are subordinated because of their sexual orientation. In fact, I was completely oblivious to the discrimination and oppression of people who are gay, lesbian, and bisexual well into adulthood.

I believe that when our teenage son confronted my husband and me as we laughed at a so-called gay joke, it was a turning point. I was no longer willing to act as though gays, lesbians, and bisexuals did not exist. The hypocrisy of struggling for the rights of women and people of color while excluding a whole segment of the population became untenable. The shift from being oblivious to being knowledgeable and caring was slow. However, I immediately stopped laughing at so-called gay "jokes." I started to think seriously about what it might be like to be gay or lesbian in a heterosexual world.

I thought back to a time in Jamaica when a friendship developed between me and a colleague who was gay identified only with his friends. He was concerned about his safety, so he was 'out' only to a small circle of people he trusted. I thought about how competent, caring, and charming he was. In conversations with him I learned that there was a large gay population in Jamaica. He assured me that I probably knew several gay men. This surprised me until he pointed out that they were closeted, and that many of them were married to women. As I reflected on this relationship with a gay man, it occurred to me that I needed to reach out to people who are gay and lesbian. I was fortunate that at about this time, a lesbian and a gay man became members of our consulting network. Their acceptance of who they were, their courage in challenging us as heterosexuals, combined with their fearlessness in addressing issues of prejudice and discrimination for not only gays and lesbians, but for women and people of color as well in our client systems, greatly accelerated my learning.

By the time Jamie joined our professional network, I had become a supportive ally in the struggle for gay and lesbian rights. Nevertheless, I know that homophobia, like sexism or racism, is too deeply entrenched to completely disappear. I have a colleague who says, *"This stuff is embedded in our spines."* I think that the best that I can do, however, is to monitor my thoughts and my behavior and, above all, keep my heart and mind open and receptive to learning.

I remember how nervous I was as the day for my dialogue with Jamie approached. He was kind enough to come over to my home. My husband and I offered him a lunch of Jamaican "jerk" chicken. I prayed that neither of us would inadvertently say nor do anything that might upset Jamie. Lunch went off smoothly, and then we had our dialogue.

CLOSING REFLECTIONS

Jamie's focus from the outset was on the impact of HIV/AIDS in the black community, and its impact on black men in particular. This was the issue that was uppermost in his mind. It's important to remind the reader that in the Dialogue model, the subordinated group member—in this case, Jamie—had the authority to decide on the aspect of LGBT life that he would share. As a heterosexual, and therefore the dominant group member in the dialogue, my primary job was to listen, to try to understand Jamie's reality, and to support him to tell his story as fully as he might choose. It was also my job to share the feelings evoked in me by Jamie's disclosures, and most of all to recognize that he was offering me the gift of learning something new.

My colleague Dr. Kathy Obear,[1] who kindly reviewed my book, pointed out that an unintended impact of our dialogue could be that some readers may be reinforced in their belief that AIDS is a gay disease, or that men on the "down low" are to be blamed for the spread of HIV/AIDS. Unfortunately, these stereotypes of gay men of all races, and gay black men in particular, are not uncommon in the heterosexual community.

So it's important to reiterate that this was not an interview. In a typical interview, the scope of the conversation would have been broader. I was interested in hearing and learning about the experience of gays who are white, as well as the experience of people who are lesbian and bisexual across racial lines. I was also interested in learning about aspects of life for LGBT people that go beyond the impact of HIV/AIDS. As the heterosexual and dominant group member, however, I could not dictate what our focus would be. This is a good demonstration of the fact that the Dialogue with Difference model grants that decision-making power and authority to the subordinated group member. So Jamie spoke from his heart about issues and experiences that were currently causing him the most concern.

As I listened to him I realized that I, a black heterosexual woman, seldom thought about HIV/AIDS. I was, however, aware that the disease was taking a serious toll across all demographics, and certainly across race and sexual orientation. From time to time I would read an article in a magazine or newspaper, or I would react to some statistics about the impact of the HIV virus in Africa. I have been concerned for some time about the spread of the virus among African American heterosexual women. But in terms of my day-to-day life, the impact of AIDS on the gay or heterosexual community was seldom on my screen. In conversations with my presumed heterosexual friends, this was seldom ever a topic. We are not callous people immune to the suffering of others, but we had somehow insulated ourselves from this disease that has been killing both people who are homosexual and heterosexual and undermining communities since the early '80s.

For Jamie, like so many gay men, this was not some distant issue. For Jamie, AIDS represented devastation and loss that I personally had not experienced.

The overall impact of my dialogue with Jamie is that it reminded me of my unconsciousness as a dominant group member. This is the reality of being part of a dominant group. We unconsciously create a world that works for us and precludes the reality of others. I am a subordinated group member in terms of my race, my gender, and my national origin. So, not surprisingly, I see and experience the world largely from the perspective of subordinated groups. However, I am also a member of dominant groups in terms of sexual orientation

CLOSING REFLECTIONS

and religion. My dominant group memberships as heterosexual and Christian are helping me to understand how it is possible for whites to be unconscious and unaware of racial disparities and discrimination, as well as how it is possible for men to be unaware of the frustrations and grief of women living in a male-dominated world. This window into the experience of dominant groups is helping me to relinquish judgment and to replace it with compassion. We really are all in this mess together.

Jamie also talked about the gender confusion that gay men experience. This led me to ponder the rigidly defined gender identities and gender roles and expression that dominant group members have created. This has resulted in so much confusion and pain, not only for homosexual men and women, but also for heterosexual women and men. When a heterosexual man quits his job, and chooses instead to do housework and care for his child, he risks being "accused" of being gay. After all, in a male-dominated world, child rearing and housework are supposed to be the domain of women. Women leaders in the workplace who are smart and tough are often referred to as "dykes." They are not perceived to be "real women," so they must be lesbian—that is, "women wanting to be men." Somehow, in our limited, heterosexual worldview, there is an inconsistency between being feminine, and being smart and tough. Heterosexual men who are presumed to be gay because of what homophobic heterosexuals perceive to be their feminine mannerisms have been beaten up and even killed. So the roots of homophobia extend to what dominants see as the feminine in men and the masculine in women. Suzanne Pharr, activist and author, expands on this thought:

> Gay men are perceived also as a threat to male dominance and control, and the homophobia expressed against them has the same roots in sexism as does homophobia against

lesbians. Visible gay men are the objects of extreme hatred and fear by heterosexual men because their breaking ranks with male heterosexual solidarity is seen as a damaging rent in the very fabric of sexism. They are seen as betrayers, as traitors who must be punished and eliminated. In the beating and killing of gay men we see clear evidence of this hatred. When we see the fierce homophobia expressed toward gay men, we can begin to understand the ways sexism also affects males through imposing rigid, dehumanizing gender roles on them.[2]

I grieved for Jamie when he talked about gays losing family and friends because of their sexual orientation. This triggered memories of an incident that occurred in a workshop a few years ago. We were exploring sexual orientation, and resistance to the topic was intense. A white man who I'll call Bob said, *"I come from a very religious family. When my sister told us that she was lesbian, we essentially banished her from our family. I haven't seen her or spoken to her in twenty years."*

My heart nearly stopped beating when he said this. I thought about the pain this rift must have caused not only for his sister, but for him and their family as well. As the challenging discussion progressed, Bob said, *"I don't approve of the lifestyle of homosexuals, but I don't think that they should be discriminated against at work."*

This gave me the opening I needed. I leaned forward in my chair and asked Bob, *"Given everything we have talked about this evening, would you consider calling your sister?"* He looked at me as if I had lost my mind. *"Absolutely not,"* he said. *"Given the way we have treated her I am sure she wouldn't want to hear from me."* I took a deep breath and said, *"I am not so sure about that, Bob. Something tells me that your sister has been waiting for your call for twenty years."* He just looked at me, but didn't respond.

CLOSING REFLECTIONS

At the start of the final day of the workshop, Bob said:

"I have something to say to the group. Against my better judgment, I called my sister. Nothing prepared me for her reaction. She was so happy to hear from me. She said that all was forgiven. We talked for over an hour. We cried and laughed together. We plan to meet in two weeks."

I wasn't the only person in that room with tears in my eyes. What I pray for in these discussions about difference is that some healing might occur. I was grateful for Bob's courage in reaching out to his sister. I was equally grateful for her compassionate spirit, and her willingness to forgive the incalculable harm that had been done to her by her own family.

In our dialogue, Jamie and I also talked about the intersection of race and sexual orientation. We both recognized that blacks who are homosexual suffer the double whammy of racism and heterosexism. Women of color who are lesbian are also dealing with the added burdens of racism and sexism. What is most painful, however, is that black, Latino, or Asian homosexuals, like their white counterparts, are often banished not only by their communities, but by their families as well. So the isolation of homosexuals of color is pretty overwhelming. As organizational consultant and author Heather Wishik notes:

> For people of color there is no guarantee of welcome and support from the white-dominated gay, lesbian, and bisexual community; ...The risk of coming out for people of color thus includes lack of a gay, lesbian, or bisexual community to come out into and loss of "home," one's own cultural community, which leaves only the "hostile white world."[3]

What is the impact on you of what you have read so far, I wonder? I hope that I've been able to convey the painful and challenging reality of prejudice and discrimination. I know that there are many who believe that sexual orientation is a choice. I stopped believing this when I realized that, as a heterosexual, I had not chosen my sexual orientation. What I recall is that boys were disgusting until some kind of transformation occurred at about age thirteen. Suddenly those same boys became really cute. There was no conscious decision on my part to become a heterosexual. Rather, it was a natural process. I grew into a woman who was attracted to the opposite sex. It seems reasonable to believe that gays, bisexuals, and lesbians evolved in similar fashion. Also, given the reality of homophobia, would anyone really choose to be homosexual? Would anyone risk being banished from a loving family? Would anyone risk being a social outcast? Would anyone risk violent attacks and the possibility of being murdered?

I have believed for some years that there is a continuum of sexual orientation. Heterosexuals are at one end of this continuum, and homosexuals at the opposite end. There is a range of orientations between the two. According to the American Psychological Association, "Research over decades has demonstrated that sexual orientation ranges along a continuum, from exclusive attraction to the other sex to exclusive attraction to the same sex."[4]

I think it is fair to conclude that human beings cannot be rigidly categorized in terms of their sexual orientation. Nevertheless, heterosexuals as a dominant group cling to the belief that all human beings should be heterosexual, and that homosexuality is a chosen lifestyle not a valid group identity. Despite evidence to the contrary, we continue trying to fit people into boxes with finite labels.

CLOSING REFLECTIONS

As I reflect on my life, I realize that I've been secure in the fact that I am heterosexual and not "one of them," i.e., not a lesbian, a member of a despised group. So it was a little unnerving when, in my early thirties and early forties, a couple of women on separate occasions seemed to have thought that I was lesbian. On one occasion I was with my husband and preteen children in a nightclub at a family resort in Montego Bay. I was surprised to say the least when a woman tourist asked me to dance. This didn't have much impact. I simply thought it was odd that a woman wanted to dance with me. In Jamaica, women did not dance with women. My husband said that she was probably lesbian. I was a little disturbed by her invitation, but I shrugged my shoulders and moved on. The other incident occurred when I was consulting to an organization in the Caribbean. One of the women on staff there had been very supportive and helpful with the project I was working on. I was delighted when she invited me to lunch at her home. As soon as we arrived, she excused herself and then returned to the living room dressed in a mini cotton robe. I thought that this was very odd given that this was the middle of the workday. We talked about work-related issues over lunch, but I felt extremely uncomfortable and could hardly wait for lunch to end.

As I look back on these situations, I recall that there was no explicit sexual invitation. Yet I believed that a lesbian had approached me at an intimate level. There was no conversation with any of the women about what, if anything had happened. I moved on with my life without giving these incidents any thought whatsoever. In retrospect, I am struck by the fact that I wasn't flattered by these approaches. Instead, my reaction was one of fear, fear at the thought of being assumed to be lesbian. I am grateful to Dr. Kathy Obear for pointing out that at an unconscious level I may have perceived lesbians to be sexual predators. This, after all, is a common stereotype of lesbians by heterosexuals. I recognize that my reaction was not atypical to that of heterosexual women who had not yet confronted their own homophobia. Occasionally in workshops, some presumed heterosexual women have admitted that fear of being assumed to be lesbian has kept them quiet in the face of prejudice against people who are lesbian, gay, bisexual or transgender. Now that I've been on a path that is helping me learn about my prejudices and biases regarding homosexuality, and what it means to be a heterosexual, I am truly shocked that I treated these incidents with such indifference and disdain. It seems that my heterosexual dominance was like an impregnable wall that shielded me from the desire for conversation or introspection or even simple human connection. Author Suzanne Pharr sheds some light on this deeply rooted fear that heterosexual women have of being assumed to be lesbian:

> To be a lesbian is to be perceived as someone who has stepped out of line, who has moved out of sexual/economic dependence on a male, who is woman-identified. A lesbian is perceived as someone who can live without a man and who is therefore (however illogically) against men. A lesbian is perceived as being outside the acceptable, routinized order of things. She is seen as someone who has no societal institutions to protect her and who is not privileged to the protection of individual males. Many heterosexual women see her as someone who stands in contradiction to the sacrifices they have made to conform to compulsory heterosexuality. A lesbian is perceived as a threat to the nuclear family, to male dominance and control, to the very heart of sexism.[5]

As a young woman, did I know this at some unconscious level? Is that why I ran metaphorically from even thinking about these incidents in which I was mistaken for a lesbian?

Fortunately, in the United States today, one can find examples of self-identified lesbians in many spheres of national life. These are powerful women in leadership roles who made the decision to come out of the closet and self-identify as lesbian. I think of Ellen Degeneres, who was courageous enough to risk losing her talk show on network television. She lost her original show, but her talent and grace triumphed, because she is back on another network with a highly rated show. I think of Rachel Maddow, Ph.D., Rhodes scholar, political analyst, and one of the most powerful opinion makers on television. She speaks her truth fearlessly. I think of women worldwide who have left the financial and social security of marriage to live openly or discreetly as lesbians. These are audacious women who have chosen to live authentically, despite the strictures of society. Adrienne Rich gives us a glimpse of what it is like to liberate yourself as lesbian:

> I have an indestructible memory of walking along a particular block in New York City, the hour after I had acknowledged to myself that I loved a woman, feeling invincible. For the first time in my life I experienced sexuality as clarifying my mind instead of hazing it over; that passion, once named, flung a long, imperative beam of light into my future. I knew my life was decisively and forever different; and that change felt to me like power.[6]

Beth Brant described her experience of coming out in this way: "I feel a sense of relief, a sense of joy, I'm an outlaw that just escaped the posse! I became a lesbian tonight."[7]

Many gays and lesbians over the years have told me how frightening it was to be afraid of who they were. They knew at a very young age that they were "different," but they didn't know what it meant to be "different." Many have talked about how hurtful and debilitating it was to hear their beloved parents and siblings make disparaging remarks about homosexuals. Many gay men report the awful experience of being called "queer, pansy, or faggot" by their classmates. Young lesbians, long before they knew the word "lesbian," heard certain women described as "dykes" or "butch." There was the sense that there was something wrong with these women. The fact that there were no openly lesbian or gay people in their families, or in their communities, deepened their feelings of insecurity and fear. There were no role models to visibly demonstrate that it was okay for them to be bisexual, lesbian, or gay. There were no role models to show them that they could grow up and be happy and successful. According to theorist Anthony D'Augelli:

> The "hidden curriculum" of heterosexism is taught to all, even those children who as adults will self-identify as lesbian/gay and bisexual. In contrast to other groups, lesbians, gay men, and bisexual people have grown up absorbing a destructive mythology before they appreciate that it is meant for them. Homophobia at such an early age is unusually resistant to change.[8]

As I mentioned in my dialogue with Jamie, I have three grandchildren whom I love deeply. What if it turns out that my grandson is gay, bisexual, or transgender, or that my granddaughters are lesbian, transgender, or bisexual? I know that I will simply continue to love them as the wonderful human beings that they are. If they had been born twenty-five years ago, I don't know that I could have made that statement. My own homophobia would not have allowed it. I know that when my children or my grandchildren were born, I never thought about their sexual orientation. Like other members of

CLOSING REFLECTIONS

my family, I made the unconscious assumption that they were heterosexual. I often think about my spiritual responsibility as a grandparent, a parent, a sibling, an aunt, a friend, a colleague. Do I accept all sexual orientations as valid, or do I treat some human beings as if they are not fully human? In relation to sexual orientation, what kind of atmosphere do I create by what I say or don't say? Do others with whom I interact know, by what I say and do that I accept and embrace all sexual orientations? Do I unwittingly inflict psychological pain and hurt by continuing to act as if everyone is heterosexual? Have I thought about the impact on closeted lesbians, gays, and bisexuals when I make an assumption of heterosexuality? Have I thought about the impact on heterosexuals when I make an assumption that everyone around me is heterosexual? I hope that readers are willing to ponder these questions, and that you may have generated some questions of your own.

I had been working on issues of diversity for a number of years before I really understood that the dynamics of all the "isms"—sexism, racism, heterosexism, ageism, etc.—parallel each other. For instance, if you are a heterosexual woman struggling for justice and equality, understand that LGBT people have similar goals. If you are a person of color wondering if barriers based on race will ever be eliminated, understand that gays, lesbians, bisexuals, and transgender people of all races, also want to be treated with the respect and dignity that every human being deserves. If you are over fifty, and you are being sidelined at work despite your considerable skills and experience, or if you are living with a physical disability and you are being denied access to opportunity, consider the following: LGBT people share your desire to be recognized as competent, caring individuals who can contribute positively in the community or in the organization. The struggle of women, people of color, LGBTs, older people, disabled people, immigrants is ultimately the same struggle. It's a struggle for acceptance. It's a struggle for human rights.

Suzanne Pharr makes the point succinctly:

> It is virtually impossible to view one oppression, such as sexism, or homophobia, in isolation because they are all connected: sexism, racism, homophobia, classism, ableism, anti-Semitism, ageism. They are linked by a common origin—economic power and control—and by common methods of limiting, controlling, and destroying lives.[9]

In closing, *"What would you do if you were not afraid?"* This was a powerful question asked by consultant Heather Wishik, who is a self-identified lesbian, at an IBM conference for gay, lesbian, and bisexual employees a few years ago. I have tried to keep that question in the front of my mind because it helps me remain true to my values of social justice and equality.

If you are heterosexual, what would you do if you were not afraid? Here are some specific questions for you to ponder:

Would you invite an out lesbian colleague to lunch with the rest of your pals? Would you read other books that help you learn about issues of sexual orientation? Would you explore your own biases and prejudices about LGBT people? Would you initiate a conversation with a self-identified lesbian, gay, or bisexual about her/his life experience? Would you speak up when someone in your family or at work makes a so-called joke that is disrespectful of gays? Would you support the right of LGBT people to adopt children and to marry? Would you write to your congressional representative about the need for a federal

CLOSING REFLECTIONS

anti discrimination law that protects this subordinated group? Would you explore what it means to be heterosexual? Whether you are white or of color, would you consider that your racial biases might also be a hindrance to relationships with LGBT people? If you are a black heterosexual, are you concerned about homophobia in the black community? What would you do if you were not afraid?

If you are lesbian, gay, bisexual, or transgender, what would you do if you were not afraid? Here are some specific questions for you to ponder:

Would you find the courage to come out of the closet? Would you speak out against harassment and discrimination of LGBTs? Would you explore the self-hatred you may have absorbed from living in a heterosexist society? Would you stop colluding with heterosexuals who are openly biased against your group? Whether you are white or of color, would you explore your own racial prejudices and biases? If you are white, would you become an ally with LGBTs of color in your mutual struggle for justice? Would you be willing to dialogue with a concerned but inept heterosexual about the reality of being gay, bisexual, or lesbian? Would you participate in your company's efforts to develop an inclusive environment for LGBTs and for all employees? What would you do if you were not afraid?

A quote that is attributed to the late Audre Lorde, Caribbean American black lesbian and feminist is fitting: "…while we wait in silence for that final luxury of fearlessness, the weight of that silence will choke us."

As I was completing my revisions of the manuscript, the chairman of the Joint Chiefs of Staff of the armed forces of the United

States, Admiral Mike Mullen, was testifying before the Senate Armed Services Committee on the military's 'Don't Ask, Don't Tell' policy. I sat in awe as I heard him say loudly and clearly:

> No matter how I look at this issue, I cannot escape being troubled by the fact that we have in place a policy which forces young men and women to lie about who they are in order to defend their fellow citizens. For me personally, it comes down to integrity—theirs as individuals and ours as an institution.[10]

When Senator Jeff Sessions of Alabama accused Admiral Mullen of "undue command influence," he replied, "This is not about command influence; this is about leadership, and I take that very seriously."

I was deeply moved by the admiral's courage, by his understanding that leaders have a moral responsibility to themselves and to the nation to do what they believe is right, regardless of fierce opposition and regardless of the consequences to them personally. In this moment, I saw some of what is best in my adopted country. Admiral Mullen has signaled to the military, and to the society at large, that we must dismantle the policies and practices that deny human rights to people who are lesbian, gay, bisexual or transgender. He was pointing the way forward to the new frontier.

※ ※ ※

Postscript: On Saturday, December 18, 2010 the United States Senate repealed the 'Don't Ask, Don't Tell' policy. I am beginning to feel that the new frontier is within reach.

APPENDIX A

COMMON SCENARIOS
TEN POSSIBLE RESPONSES FOR
CONCERNED HETEROSEXUALS

1. A manager who reports to you says: "Homosexuals are sinners and their behavior is deviant and unnatural." You want to respond: "You are homophobic!"

Try not to accuse someone of being homophobic—unless you want to shut down the conversation and possibly lose a productive colleague or friend. Once I made that mistake with a new client. He was furious with me and nearly threw me out of his office. Now that may have been an accurate statement on my part, but what's the point of being "right" if the result is that you have closed the door to dialogue? Instead, you could respond, *"Help me understand why you feel that way."* Better yet, *"How do you think your perspective impacts LGBT people in our organization?"* That could have led into a great discussion about the ways in which he could support the company's values on fairness and equality for all employees, including LGBTs. That would also have been recognition that at the end of the day, the actions he takes as a manager are more important than what he thinks or believes about homosexuality.

2. Your teenage son says: "Mom, I think I'm gay." How might you respond?

Start by giving him a hug. Tell him how much you appreciate his honesty. Tell him you love him. Then engage him in conversation. For example: *"What makes you think you are gay?"* Given the homophobia of the world in which he is growing up, disclosing that he is gay takes a lot of courage. It may have scared him to discover that he is gay. If he has picked up that either of his parents is prejudiced against LGBT people, he will be even more frightened. He doesn't know how you will react, and he has heard that some parents have actually thrown their gay and lesbian kids out of their home. Most of all he wants to believe that you will continue to love him for who he is. A gay friend told me that he knew he was gay from when he was very young. Initially, he was too scared to tell his parents, so he told his grandparents instead. They embraced him and continued to love him unconditionally. He said he doesn't know how he could have coped without their support. So it's important to recognize that despite his fear, your son trusts that you will not reject him. Let him know that you will always be there for him. Keep his disclosure a secret if he asks you to. If his decision is to be "out" to other family members, tell him that you will support him. Consider joining PFLAG—Parents, Families, and Friends of Lesbians and Gays, a support organization. Because he has trusted you with his big secret, a special bond now exists between you and your son. Be grateful for it. This scenario is also applicable if your teenage daughter tells you she is lesbian, bisexual, or transgender.

3. A kid in your classroom says: *"I've heard that some kids are being harassed because they are gay, lesbian, or transgender."* How might you respond?

"I want all of you kids to know that if any of you are being teased or harassed for any reason, I want to know about it. I am so distressed about the reports in the media about gay, lesbian, or transgender children who have committed suicide in order to escape the stress of being teased and harassed by classmates. I never want to see that happen to any child in our school. So I have decided to create a safe environment for LGBT kids. You know where to find me. I promise that I will always find time to talk with you."

Consider initiating conversations with kids about the destructive impact of prejudice and hate. Help them understand that both perpetrators and victims suffer. Try to get more specific information from the child who reported what she had heard. Talk with other teachers about effective ways of supporting these at risk LGBT kids. Immediately report to your principal any cases of harassment that come to your attention.

4. A lesbian couple has moved in next door. A friend says, *"I hear you have some dykes with kids next door. Our neighborhood is going to hell. What if they influence our kids to become gay?"* How might you respond?

"I must admit I wasn't thrilled about having lesbians as my next-door neighbors, but I've met Jean and Diane, and they really seem to be nice people. Do you really think that our neighborhood is going to hell? What do you think might actually happen?"

Continue to engage your friend in dialogue. Then try to listen without judgment to what your friend has to say. You may continue: *"Do you really think that somebody could influence you to become a lesbian? Of course I don't have proof, but more and more I believe that people are born either 'straight' or gay."* Depending on where you are in your own journey of awareness and acceptance, you may need to try hard not to explode in anger or to launch an attack. At some point in your conversation, you may want to tell your friend that you plan to invite your new neighbors over for coffee.

5. Your dad tells a so-called gay joke in front of your kids. How might you respond?

"Dad, that is so inappropriate. I am doing everything I can to bring my kids up without prejudice or fear of other people. Don't ever make a so-called gay joke in my home again." A dear friend told me recently that he had made a similar mistake when he was visiting his son and grandkids. He said that when his son reprimanded him, he was shocked, and that it felt like a slap in the face. Having thought about it, however, he now feels new respect for his son for the stand that he is taking. He also decided that it was time for him to pay more attention to his prejudices about people who are lesbian, gay, bisexual, or transgender. Sometimes directness is the best option.

6. A colleague asks, *"Why can't they keep their sexual orientation to themselves? We shouldn't be talking about sex at work."* How might you respond?

"You know, I really don't think it's about sex. I think that LGBT people are as concerned about prejudice and discrimination in the workplace as we women are. That's why they are 'coming out,' and that's why they have formed a support group. So it's not about sex. Do you think it's fair that some people don't get the coaching they need to succeed, or the promotions they deserve, because of their sexual orientation? I know how strongly you feel about gender bias here at work. I am seriously

thinking about joining the LGBT support group as a heterosexual ally. Do you think I'm crazy?"

7. A family member says, *"Why do they want to get married? Marriage is a sacred institution for heterosexuals."* How might you respond?

"I imagine they want to marry because they are in love and want to make a sacred commitment to each other. I must admit that initially I was disturbed at the thought of gay/lesbian marriage. But I am beginning to shift my position. When you stop to think about it, why should marriage be for us heterosexuals only? We don't lose anything when LGBT people marry, do we? To be honest about it, we say we believe that marriage is a sacred institution, but over 50 percent of marriages end in divorce. Some people say that another 20 percent of marriages should also end in divorce. Sometimes I think that we are being more than a little hypocritical on this issue. Also, let's not forget that there are some important legal and financial benefits from being married. Do you really think that our fellow citizens should be denied these benefits just because their sexual orientation is different to ours?"

8. Your favorite uncle says, *"The Bible is explicit about the fact that homosexuality is a sin. How could I possibly support equal rights for gays and lesbians?"* How might you respond?

"That is a difficult issue for us as Christians, isn't it? I also know that it is a challenging issue for my Muslim friends. For some time I've been wrestling with my Christian beliefs on the one hand, and my desire for a fair and just society on the other. Here are some of the things I've considered in relation to the Bible. In Exodus 35:2, it says that a neighbor who works on the Sabbath should be put to death. In Leviticus 11:10, it says that eating shellfish is an abomination. Like the verses on homosexuality, I just don't believe that those verses can be taken literally. I don't claim to have all the answers, but I can tell you that I believe that God created LGBT people

and us heterosexuals alike, in his image. My God is also a God of love. Uncle Joe, do you believe that God wants us to hate others, or to relegate them to second-class status because of who they are?"* Listen respectfully to your uncle's response. You may wish to say at some point in your conversation: *"I am also struck by the fact that sexual orientation is not mentioned in the New Testament. Jesus never said a word about it. So I will continue to reach out to people who are lesbian, gay, bisexual, or transgender, and I continue to be grateful for the friendships I have made."*

9. A close friend says, *"They just hired a gay man in my department. I'm terrified. I could get infected with HIV/AIDS."* How might you respond?

"A lot of people feel that way. But the fact is there is scientific evidence that the disease is contracted through sexual contact with someone who is infected, or through contact with infected blood, in a syringe, for example. So you can't get infected from using the same telephone or the same computer. I also try to remember that HIV or AIDS is not a gay disease. There are a lot of heterosexuals who have either the virus or the disease itself. Do you have any other concerns about working with a guy who is gay? By the way, how do you know that he is gay?"

Listen to what your friend has to say. Empathize: *"I can see that you are really worried."* Continue to say why you don't think this man's presence in your department will be a problem.

10. You are at a party with friends and someone says, *"Look at those homos, hugging and simpering. They just don't belong here."* How might you respond?

"You know, until recently, I would have reacted to Jim and John's presence exactly the way you just did. Now I feel really uncomfortable when you make

put-down remarks like that. After the diversity class that I took at work, I am really trying to pay attention to my prejudices. My eyes popped when I read the articles the trainers gave us about the oppression of LGBTs. Would you like to see the articles? I think that my greatest learning from the class was seeing, for the first time, the link between prejudice based on race, and prejudice based on sexual orientation. How many times have we heard that because we are black we don't belong? I know from the numerous conversations we've had, how concerned you are about the unjust treatment of blacks and other people of color. Would you be willing to have a conversation with me about the similar treatment of LGBT people?"

In summary: Notice the key themes that run through all of these responses:

- Finding the courage to speak up, i.e., breaking the silence that helps keep bigotry in place;
- Sharing honestly your own fears;
- Engaging others in a way that results in more dialogue;
- Being willing to listen, respectfully, to what others have to say;
- Trying consciously to suspend judgment so that you can really hear a different perspective;
- Avoiding "beating up" on others: empathizing and being compassionate with all others as well as with yourself;
- Recognizing that awareness of gender, race, religious, or other types of oppression is a gateway to building awareness about oppression based on sexual orientation.

APPENDIX B

STORIES OF PREJUDICE AND DISCRIMINATION

THE COUNTRY MOURNS

We were all shocked and horrified at the events of 9/11. People with spouses, relatives, and friends who were killed or injured continue to try to recover and to resume a life that approaches normalcy. It is likely that if we are heterosexual, we haven't thought about the impact on the lives of gays, lesbians, or bisexuals who were victims of this disaster. Many had partners, relatives, or friends who lost their lives or were injured in the resulting carnage. Where would they go to grieve? Would they be able to find financial and emotional support from local and federal authorities that played such a significant role for bereaved heterosexuals in the aftermath of the tragedy?

I am about to tell the story of a gay man, Claude, who lost his partner of seventeen years on that day that many think may have forever changed the course of American history. His partner's name was David. A close friend who had known the couple since their college years told me their story.

Claude and David moved to New Jersey in September 2000 because they both got jobs in Manhattan. They both worked, as it happens, a few blocks from the World Trade Center. When the first plane hit the tower on that fateful day, David called Claude. They were frightened, and at a loss, as they tried to figure out what was going on. They met at Claude's office and very quickly decided that it would be a good idea to get away from that section of town as rapidly as possible. They were about three blocks away from the World Trade Center when the first tower collapsed, scattering bodies, body parts, and assorted debris over a wide radius of lower Manhattan.

Moments before the collapse of the first tower, David was on the phone to his mom. He figured she might be watching the horror unfold on TV, and he wanted to assure her that he and Claude were safe. As he talked, he and Claude were holding hands tightly, and walking as fast as they could among the throngs of people trying to escape the area. As the tons of concrete and steel that formed the tower fell, Claude was thrown to the ground. He doesn't know how long he lay there, but when he got up, there was mass confusion and pandemonium. David was nowhere in sight. Claude couldn't see very well because of the clouds of dust surrounding and choking him, but he searched the area as thoroughly as he could. To his consternation and dismay, he could not find David. This made no sense to him. They had been holding hands a minute ago. They were walking side by side. How could he have disappeared?

Eventually, Claude went to the armory. David was not there. He searched the hospitals and still his beloved could not be found. Two days later, his worst fear was realized when he found David's name listed among the dead. It had been easy for the authorities to identify him, because he was carrying his driver's license in his wallet, which he had secured in his back pocket. In that moment of anguish, the kind of inane thought that often comes in times of extreme stress flashed across Claude's mind. "This is so strange," he thought. "David always carried his wallet in his briefcase, never in his pocket."

From the condition of the body, it was assumed that David must have fallen when the tower came crashing down, and that the crowd had trampled him.

Claude was devastated by the loss of his partner. He could not understand how life could go on without him. His pain became excruciating when he discovered that he was not recognized as next of kin, despite seventeen years of a monogamous relationship. Claude had no legal standing whatsoever. The basic necessity of caring for the body of your beloved, an important step in the process of grieving, was denied him. It was David's parents who had to give permission for his body to be released for burial.

This was the beginning of a downward spiral for Claude. In the short period of six months, he had lost the love of his life; he had lost his job and the beautiful home he had shared with David; and he also lost his standard of living. And he was soon to lose his mind.

His life had become a living nightmare. He could not afford to maintain the home he and David had so lovingly created with its choice antiques and exquisite artwork. The home in which they had entertained so many of their friends was now in his past. He wondered how he would live. David had been the primary income earner. With their combined income, they had enjoyed a rich and satisfying quality of life. They traveled extensively around the world, and the décor of their home reflected the arts and crafts of the many countries they had visited.

At David's funeral, Claude was inconsolable, and at times hysterical. In his eulogy he not only spoke about the love he and David had for each other, but also about the fact that as the surviving partner of a gay union, he had no rights. He had not only lost the love of his life. He had lost everything. Some of the mourners, particularly members of David's family, perceived his statements to be political and inappropriate.

Some weeks after David's funeral, Claude decided to go on a trip to Italy. He and David had started to plan this trip a few months before David died. Claude thought that getting out of town and getting out of the country for a few weeks might lift his spirits. He arrived in Rome in time for the Christmas holidays and reconnected with friends who provided him some comfort. While in Rome, he had what his friends described as a psychotic outburst. He was hospitalized and sent back to the United States heavily sedated with anti-psychotic drugs. His friends were shocked at this turn of events, because Claude did not have a history of mental illness. They wondered if the trauma he had experienced on 9/11 and its aftermath had destabilized him emotionally and mentally.

After a few weeks of psychiatric treatment, Claude appeared to be functioning well. He was getting on with his life. He had a new job, and he had found a small apartment. His friends continued to offer emotional support. Behind the scenes, however, he felt as if he were being ripped apart.

He and David had enjoyed a loving relationship with David's family. They knew that David's intent was to name his Mom and Claude equal beneficiaries of his estate. After David died, his relationship with David's family deteriorated. They accused him of wanting to appropriate all of David's estate. Legally he had no legs to stand on, because David had not completed the paperwork that would have given Claude legal ownership of his retirement funds and some property he owned. In the end, David's family took almost everything David had left behind. Claude was devastated not only because of the financial loss, but because in his mind he had been cast out by David's family, the family that had embraced him so warmly when David was alive.

The depression that had started with David's tragic death deepened. He could not concentrate on his work, and early in the New Year he lost his job. With no source of income, he moved in with his parents. Claude sank further and further into depression. The day before his fortieth birthday, he killed himself. He committed suicide in the living room of his parents' home. He butchered himself. The police who found him said that there was blood everywhere.

Claude's friends and family knew that he was depressed, but it never crossed their minds that he might take his own life. That seemed entirely out of character. The fact that he savagely mutilated himself, and died in such pain, is a horror that those who loved him will never forget.

THE DANCE OF DIFFERENCE

THE ISSUE IS TRUST

Karen, a petite white woman, was a senior statistician in a company located in the South. She was highly respected for her technical skills and her ability to be a team player in her own department as well as on the cross-functional teams created by the company. After three years in this position, she joined the diversity council. The council had been authorized by the chief executive officer and senior management to guide the company in the development of strategies that would result in a more inclusive, congenial, and productive work environment.

Karen soon became an active and dedicated member of the council, devoting time and energy to a number of committees that collaborated with senior leaders and managers in the implementation of diversity strategy. Politically she regarded herself as a liberal who had for years been concerned about issues of equity and justice for people of color, for women, and for gays, lesbians, bisexuals, and people who are transgender.

After six months on the council, she was surprised to discover that she was learning a lot about her own prejudices regarding race. She recognized that the openness of the people of color on the council was critical to her growing understanding. She was also very aware that the willingness of the women to share their experiences at work played a significant role in the increasing awareness of male members of the council about issues of gender. Karen enjoyed her job as a statistician. She felt good about the fact that both the council and company leaders shared her own personal values. As she told council members in a recent meeting, "I think that I am very fortunate to work for a company that has similar values to my own.

I really do believe that the sky is the limit for me and for any employee who is a competent performer and who supports the company's vision of inclusion."

Council members were delighted to have a hard worker like Karen on board. They admired her for her honesty, her courage, and her willingness to make herself vulnerable by talking about her racial prejudices. As the months passed and the council developed as a cohesive, high-functioning team, Karen became increasingly uncomfortable about the fact that there was an important secret that she had not shared.

After she had been on the council for about a year, the members and senior leaders participated in a one-day workshop on sexual orientation. All year long, she had been thinking that she needed to "come out of the closet," but she was terrified at the prospect. How would the council members react? Would they continue to accept her as a valuable member? What impact might this have on her career? While she knew that her company's policy required inclusion of people who were LGBT, she was also aware of the high level of homophobia among company employees. She was also concerned about homophobia in society in general, and particularly concerned about homophobia in the South. However, she was at the point where she felt that her personal integrity required that she "come out" to the council as a lesbian.

During a discussion in which council members and management shared their concern that there were so few gay/lesbian/bisexual employees who felt safe enough to "come out," Karen, to her own surprise, said, "I know why it is so difficult for folks to disclose their sexual orientation. I know that we have a policy of inclusion, and I honestly believe that our leaders are sincere in their commitment.

However, it is still hard to trust that if you are lesbian or gay, you will continue to be treated with respect. It is not easy to risk jeopardizing your career. I know what I am talking about, because I am a lesbian. I hope that you can forgive me for being silent about this for so long, but even in this moment I can't tell you how afraid I am." For a few seconds after Karen spoke, there was total silence in the room. Then several council members and managers assured Karen that she would continue to have their support, and that they admired her courage in speaking out. Karen's relief was intense. She realized that even though she was still afraid, she felt as if a great burden had rolled off of her shoulders.

Within a few days, she came out to her manager and to her colleagues. She was relieved to discover that most members of her work group seemed to be fairly comfortable with her disclosure. In a matter of months, Karen became an outspoken leader on issues of sexual orientation in the company and she joined the gay, lesbian, and bisexual network.

A few months after she had come out as lesbian, she attended an off-site meeting of one of the cross functional teams on which she worked. That night, as she was walking towards her car in the hotel parking lot, she was horrified to discover that her tires had been slashed. Over the next months, she received e-mails describing her and other homosexuals as sinful and wicked. The writers of these e-mails denounced the company for including sexual orientation in its diversity work. The CEO responded by sending out a letter reiterating the company's commitment to valuing all sexual orientations. He stated clearly that attacks on gay, lesbian, or bisexual employees could result in termination if the perpetrators were caught.

Karen learned to manage her fear. She deeply valued the heterosexuals who spoke up on her behalf and on behalf of other gay and lesbian employees. She decided that she would continue, despite the harassment, to be a spokesperson on issues of sexual orientation, as well as on race and gender.

After two years as a member of the council, Karen was voted unanimously as chairperson. The CEO and senior managers congratulated her and promised their full support. A few months previously, the company had embarked on a strategy to reduce expenses, and a small percentage of employees were let go. Karen was stunned when she was reassigned to another city. She never stopped wondering whether the fact that a lesbian was about to assume the position of chairperson of the council was the primary reason for her transfer. Her colleagues on the council were as skeptical as she was on this issue.

IN THE CLOSET

Ella grew up in a middle-class household with loving and supportive parents. She was a hard-working, brilliant student. After graduation, she joined a leading pharmaceutical company and over the years earned the reputation of excellence as a researcher. She in due course became a department head and discharged her responsibilities as manager with skill and compassion.

She fell in love with Jack, married in her late twenties, and soon gave birth to a son. She cared deeply for her husband, but as the years passed she realized that she was becoming increasingly uncomfortable, particularly with the sexual aspect of their relationship. It got to the point where she was relieved when her husband came home exhausted from work, because she knew that sex would not be on his agenda for that evening. Frequently when he tried to make love to her, she avoided intimacy by saying that she had a headache or that she was exhausted.

For some time she had begun to suspect that she was a lesbian. This possibility terrified her. She had been brought up to believe that homosexuality was a sin against God and man. Her parents were very conservative and traditional. She dared not imagine how they might react if they suspected that their only child was a lesbian. She was also beginning to admit to herself that she was attracted to women.

The tension between Ella and her husband, Jack, continued to escalate and erupted in frequent fights over the most inconsequential issues. Ella's nerves were shot, and Jack recognized that he was losing the love of his life. He begged her to tell him what was wrong, but she could only shake her head miserably and reply, "Nothing. Just be patient with me, Jack. I promise you everything will soon be okay." Eventually Jack ceased all efforts at lovemaking with Ella. Their household became more peaceful while their relationship became more strained. After months of abstinence, Jack was really suffering.

One night he said, "Ella, we've got to talk. I can't take this anymore. It's obvious that you no longer love me. Are you having an affair?" "No, Jack, there is no one else. I don't know what's wrong with me. All I know is that I need to be on my own. I am so sorry. I never meant to hurt you, but I think that separation would be the best thing for both of us." They both wept and hugged each other. Within a year they were divorced and had agreed to joint custody of their son.

Ella took a job in another city. She hated being separated from her son, but she knew that she needed time and space to start over and to resolve her conflicts regarding her sexual orientation. She went into therapy, and over the course of a year she gradually accepted the reality that she was indeed lesbian. She fell in love with a wonderful woman, Lisa, who was a physician with her own medical practice. She was happier than she had ever been as an adult. Nevertheless, she did not disclose to her family or to old friends that she was lesbian. She kept her own apartment despite the fact that her lover had asked her to move in with her. Lisa had created a beautiful home in a neighbourhood where many gay couples lived. By continuing to live in her own apartment, Ella avoided awkward questions when her son came to visit. Her biggest fear was that if she came out of the closet, her ex-husband would sue for sole custody of their son. She vowed that she would do whatever it took to maintain her role as an active parent to her son.

At work, she had become, at the request of her manager, a member of the diversity council. She participated in a diversity workshop that focused on issues of sexual orientation, race, and gender and was profoundly moved by what she learned. She was very aware of gender issues, but had never ever thought about her own racial prejudices and biases as a white woman. She listened very keenly and with great dismay as the "out" gay man and lesbian participants talked about their many negative experiences at work. On the last day she told a member of the workshop staff that she was a lesbian, and begged her never to reveal her secret. "Under no circumstances will I come out at work. I think it would be the end of my career. Despite the company's commitment to diversity, I see signs of homophobia everywhere, and I will not put myself at risk."

In her personal life Ella had found satisfaction and joy. She and her partner Lisa were deeply in love, and they had committed themselves to each other. Their only point of friction was that Ella could not bring herself to introduce Lisa as her partner to either her family or co-workers. Meanwhile, Lisa had proudly introduced Ella to her family and close friends.

Life at work was becoming increasingly difficult. Ella had become a champion on issues of gender and race, but she continued to stifle herself on the issue of sexual orientation. She wished with all her heart that she could speak out, but she did not have the courage. She just could not put her son, her career, or her personal safety at risk. Her co-workers made the assumption that she was heterosexual, and from time to time they told so-called gay jokes. They also expressed the view that the company should never have included sexual orientation in their diversity work. Ella was deeply hurt and very angry when her heterosexual co-workers expressed their contempt and disdain for lesbian, gay, and bi-sexual people. But she never said a word in response. She realized that by staying silent, she was colluding in her own oppression. Ella felt that she was caught between a rock and a hard place. Her silence was a burden that was almost unbearable. For her, coming out was not an option. She would not risk losing her son, her family, or her career.

PREJUDICES DIE HARD

Sheila, a black Caribbean American woman, was telling her friend Harris, an out gay man, how shocked she was to discover that her prejudices about gay men not only continued unabated, but that they were so close to the surface. She described an experience she had had in San Diego recently. She was in a limousine on her way to a university in the city to give a lecture on issues of oppression. Her car pulled up to the traffic light, and in the next lane there was this bright yellow convertible being driven by a white man dressed in a shirt of improbably vivid colors. He was wearing a straw hat with a bright red bandana tied around the brim. Sheila said that she looked at him, and before she could blink this thought ran through her mind: "There goes another one of those damn gays." In a less than a minute, she was horrified at herself. "Dear God," she thought, "where did that come from? I have worked so hard to move beyond the prejudices that I learned so early in life. I have gay colleagues and friends that I genuinely love and respect, and despite all of that I am still capable of this kind of vicious thinking. This is the kind of thing that makes me despair."

Harris took a deep breath and said, "I really appreciate your honesty in sharing that story with me. Does it make me feel good to know that you are capable of that kind of stereotyping and prejudice? No, it doesn't. But it's reality. As a gay man, do I understand that kind of prejudice? Not really. However, as a white man, I know that sometimes, horrible thoughts go through my mind about black people, for no other reason than the fact that they are black. So I guess I have learned what you know as well as I do. We will be working on these prejudices until we die."

"So you don't hate me?" Sheila asked anxiously. "No, of course not," said Harris. You work harder on your prejudices regarding sexual orientation than anyone I know." "Harris," Sheila said, "you have so much love in your heart, even for people who revile you, that sometimes it scares me. It's been a hard thing for me to learn, but I really am trying to be gentle with myself, to be compassionate with myself, and above all to forgive myself."

"Welcome to the club of human experience," Harris said gently. "We are all in this boat together, aren't we?"

THE DANCE OF DIFFERENCE

RESISTANCE TO CHANGE

PL&P was a public utility in the northeast part of the country. The organization was predominantly white, and the majority of people of color were concentrated in low-level jobs. One African American man had made it into the ranks of management. Several people of color had filed grievances claiming that they had been overlooked for promotions because of race prejudice. Eventually a class-action lawsuit claiming large-scale racial discrimination was filed against the company. Within months, white women had started to organize, and there were rumours that they too were planning a class-action lawsuit claiming gender discrimination. This was a wakeup call for the board of directors, the CEO, and the senior leadership team. They decided that it was time to call in a consulting firm to help them address issues of racism and sexism within the company.

Having completed an employee survey that specified a range of race, gender, and class issues, the company decided that it needed a diversity council that would assist senior management in devising strategies for change. When the company asked employees to volunteer for membership on the council, Rob, the only out gay man, in the organization, quickly volunteered and was accepted as a member.

He had no idea about the difficult negotiations that had taken place at the level of the CEO and senior leadership team regarding the inclusion of sexual orientation in the company's diversity work. Several members of the team openly and passionately opposed it. Many others were at best ambivalent. There was, however, one powerful member of the team, the vice president for construction (engineering), who spoke up passionately for the inclusion of sexual orientation at the outset. He was surprised and delighted when he received the support of their chief legal counsel. "I agree with John that there are strong ethical, moral, and business reasons for including sexual orientation in our diversity work. I am also concerned about the legal aspect. I really believe that if we exclude sexual orientation, we can expect someone to file a lawsuit against the company."

The team reluctantly and with great apprehension agreed.

The council participated in an awareness workshop with the senior leadership team. The dialogue on gender and race issues was difficult, painful, and enlightening. When the group started its work on sexual orientation, the atmosphere in the conference room became explosive. A level of hostility that had not been present earlier had crept into the discussions, as some members of both the council and the leadership team vented their prejudices and biases against gay, lesbian, and bisexual people. Other members of the council and leadership team made it clear that they would champion the work on sexual orientation as well as the work on race, gender and class. It became very clear to Rob that he had his work cut out for him. Far from being dismayed, however, he was even more determined to be an active member of the council. He also knew that he would continue to speak out on the issues whenever an opportunity presented itself.

The council agreed to meet monthly, and several members warmly welcomed Rob. They admitted that they had not thought much about sexual orientation, but as a result of the workshop, they realized that they had a great deal to learn about their own biases as heterosexuals. They also said that they were eager to hear from him about what life was like for gays and lesbians on a day-to-day basis at work.

As the months passed, a clear pattern began to emerge in council meetings. Discussions regarding race, class, and gender were difficult but congenial. However, during discussions on sexual orientation, many members were silent. Additionally, there were two members who openly said that they opposed the inclusion of sexual orientation in the company's diversity strategy. One of these members, Mark, said to Rob, "I hope you know that I don't have anything against you personally; I just can't support your lifestyle." The other member, Maria, said, "You seem to be a very nice person, but as a Christian I am obliged to speak out against our work on sexual orientation. The Bible is explicit in its statements that homosexuality is a sin, and I think that our company is wrong to force us to work on this issue."

Despite these and other attacks on his integrity as a human being, Rob never lost his cool. He said to Maria and Mark," I appreciate your being honest with me about the way you feel. My guess is that there are other members who share your views. The fact is, my sexual orientation as gay is as valid as your sexual orientation as 'straight' (heterosexual) people. I really hope that as we continue to work together, you will be able to see that the dynamics of prejudice and discrimination are essentially the same, whether the issue is gender, race, socio-economic class, or sexual orientation."

However, it soon became clear to council members that Mark and Maria had closed minds on the issue of sexual orientation. They continued to make degrading and vicious remarks about gay, lesbian, and bisexual people. Their negative attitudes began to get in the way of the work of the council. Rob continued to be patient, and to speak his truth calmly and with compassion.

After a year of conflict and little progress, the council hired consultants to help them out of the impasse in which they found themselves. The consultants organized a three-day team-building session. On the first day, an African American woman confronted Maria and Mark. Her voice was shaking as she said, "I have sat here on this council for a year and listened to the two of you repeatedly attack Rob. The hatred that I hear in your voices scares me. I want you to know that I too am a Christian, and the most important thing that I understand is that God is a God of love. He created all of us: man as well as woman; people of color as well as white; homosexuals and heterosexuals. I am proud to work for a company that is taking a stand on all of the issues that this council is asked to address. I believe strongly that every member of this council needs to support the company's vision of full inclusion for everyone regardless of race, gender, socio-economic class, or sexual orientation. If we cannot fully support the vision, then we should withdraw from the council."

Mark spoke for Maria when he replied," You have no right to attack our religious beliefs. We are deeply offended. Maria and I have decided to resign from the council. However, we want you to know that we will continue to fight the company on this issue. We are leaving, but we will not stop until the company agrees to exclude sexual orientation from its diversity strategy." With those words, Maria and Mark gathered up their belongings and walked angrily out of the conference room.

SAFETY COMES FIRST

Michael had just arrived in Baltimore to play in a major tennis tournament sponsored by a gay and lesbian tennis league. He was excited about his prospects to do well. He had put every effort into practice sessions with his coach, who he had hired specifically to prepare him for the tournament. He had also been weight training for about nine months, and he knew without question that he had improved his muscle strength as well as his endurance. He grabbed a taxi at the airport, and on their way out of the city his driver asked, "So, what brings you to Baltimore?" Without thinking, Michael replied, "I'm playing in a tennis tournament." He then recalled that the tournament had received some media coverage, so there was a possibility that the driver would know that it was a gay- and lesbian-sponsored event. He thought, "I don't know who this driver is. I'd better be careful," as the taxi moved out of the city into a more rural setting. He was frightened that he had allowed himself to become so relaxed in a homophobic world that such potentially dangerous words had passed his lips.

He was relieved that he had remembered that he might not be in a safe situation. He felt bad that he was suspicious, but the fact was that he had no idea what the driver's attitudes to gays were. Given the depth of homophobia in the society at large, why would he risk being open with a complete stranger? He wanted to believe that the possibility of some sort of violence was remote, but it was not uncommon to hear about gays and lesbians being attacked. So why take the chance?

This stance created a good deal of internal conflict for him, because he was a friendly guy who liked meeting and connecting with people. He was also very aware that each time he made the conscious choice not to be known as gay, he was colluding with his silence. In those situations he always wondered, "Did I miss an opportunity to help someone see differently?" He also thought, "For all I know, the driver might be gay and we could have a great conversation." He felt distressed and sad that he always had to pay such close attention to his boundaries. In the absence of some sure way for him to know the demarcation of those boundaries, he could only go with his gut and continue to wonder how much damage he was doing to the cause of gay liberation. He wondered about the number of relationships with gay or straight people that he may have missed. Once more he felt the enormity of the burden of always having to wonder, "Is it safe for me to be me?"

THE DANCE OF DIFFERENCE

OPEN SEASON—SHE IS A LESBIAN

Faith worked as a sales representative for a well-established pharmaceutical company in the Northeast. She was a lesbian who had never hidden her identity at work. She had been out to the rest of the world ever since she had come out to herself in her early twenties. She didn't wear her sexual orientation on her sleeve, but in her interactions with co-workers, she was naturally who she was. So, for example, she talked about what she and her partner, Jennifer, did over the weekend. When asked about the photograph of Jennifer on her desk, she would simply say, "She's my life partner."

As her mostly male colleagues realized that she was lesbian, she was pleasantly surprised and relieved to discover that they did not freak out. In fact, they seemed to accept her and were comfortable with her.

It may be helpful to say at this point that from the perspective of physical appearance, Faith was, to the average heterosexual male, a dream come true. She was a tall, willowy blond with the bluest eyes you've ever seen. She drew admiring glances wherever she went. People meeting her for the first time were invariably surprised to discover that she was not a model.

Once guys she worked with discovered that she was lesbian, the frequent response was, "You are so gorgeous, you can't possibly be lesbian." Some male colleagues went even further with demeaning remarks like, "All you need is the right guy who knows what he's doing, and Jennifer will be history." Faith found these offensive remarks extremely painful, but she tried to take them in her stride. She felt that that this kind of teasing and kidding was due to ignorance, and that there was no conscious intent to hurt her. More often than not, she ignored them or she changed the subject to some work-related issue. She was a consummate professional, and she had for some time decided that being seen as a team player was her first priority. Without that level of acceptance, it would be difficult for her to do a good job.

As time passed, however, the remarks shifted from teasing and kidding to lurid and even pornographic. Her co-workers were not only treating her as a sexual object, but it became clear that some of them felt it was appropriate to make risqué remarks. For example, "So how do you like it really? What could a woman do for you that I couldn't do better?" She was being sexually harassed and she hated it. Eventually it got to the point where some of the men would share their sexual fantasies with her. This even included their desire to have sex with two women at a time. She was genuinely shocked at this behaviour, because on the whole this was a decent group of guys. She knew that they respected her professionally because she was a good performer. Why was it so hard for them to treat her as a human being instead of as a repository for sexual obscenities? She was certainly aware that it was not unusual for lesbians to be seen by heterosexual men as sexual beings only, without a life beyond sexual activity. Given their early acceptance of her sexual orientation however, she had not anticipated that her relationships with them would descend to this level.

She used to look forward to going to work. Now each day as she arrived at the office, she wondered what titillation the guys might indulge in that day at her expense. She certainly considered confronting them and letting them know that their behaviour was inappropriate and unacceptable. But she worried that they might react by being defensive. They might even become hostile, and the good working relationships that she had worked so hard to build might disintegrate.

When she got to the point where she simply could not take it anymore, she decided that her only recourse was to go to her manager. But again, she stopped herself. She had seen him join in on the so-called jokes made about her sexual orientation. What if he did not understand the seriousness of the situation? What if he saw her as whining, versus lodging a legitimate complaint? And even if she was successful and the harassment stopped, how would the men in her group treat her? Would she continue to have the cooperation she needed to do a good job, or would they see her as a whistleblower who deserved to be isolated or treated with scorn? Faith did not know what to do with her frustration and anger. She knew that she was being exploited; yet she felt very vulnerable, because she needed her job. She felt that she was stuck between a rock and a hard place.

NOTES

Chapter I

1. The discomfort with, or the fear, hatred, or intolerance of, people who are or assumed to be gay, lesbian or bisexual.
2. Systemic oppression of people who are or are assumed to be gay, lesbian, or bisexual. The oppression is based on the assumption that heterosexuality is the best, correct, and/or preferred sexual orientation and that everyone is heterosexual. See the "Diversity Factor Language Guide 2004," Elsie Y. Cross Associates, Inc.
3. A group identity based on one's enduring emotional, romantic, affectional, and sexual attraction to members of the same or other sex.
4. A person whose primary emotional, romantic, affectional, and sexual attractions are for people of the other sex.
5. Men whose primary emotional, romantic, affectional, and sexual attractions are to other men.
6. Women whose primary emotional, romantic, affectional, and sexual attractions are for other women.
7. Persons whose primary emotional, romantic, affectional, and sexual attractions are to both women and men. See the "Diversity Factor Language Guide 2004," Elsie Y. Cross Associates, Inc.
8. Heather Wishik and Carol Pierce, *Sexual Orientation and Identity: Heterosexual, Lesbian, Gay, and Bisexual Journeys* (Laconia, NH: New Dynamics Publications, 1995).
9. Organizational development consultant, president, MGK Consulting LLC, www.mgkconsultingllc.com.
10. Wishik and Pierce, *Sexual Orientation and Identity*.

11 Terminology for LGBTs who choose not to divulge their sexual orientation.
12 Information on the status of gay marriage obtained from the Human Rights Campaign Website.

Chapter 2

1. A member of a complex black activist movement in Jamaica that originated in 1930. "Twin concepts (were) African Redemption (Repatriation to Ethiopia), and the divinity of the most revered ruler in Africa—Haile Selassie, King of Kings, the conquering lion of Judah." See Rex Nettleford, *Mirror Mirror: Identity, Race, and Protest in Jamaica* (London: Collins Clear-Type Press, 1972).
2. Hairstyle that is "a source of pride and distinction…neither combed nor cut, falling in a mass of long ringlets…tucked inside a protective tam, usually made of the Rastafarian colors—red, green, and gold." See Virginia Lee Jacobs, *Roots of Rastafari* (Avant Books, 1985).
3. See NCAVP report "Hate Violence against Lesbian, Gay, Bisexual, and Transgender People in the United States—2008." NCAVP "is a network of over thirty-five anti-violence organizations that monitor, respond to, and work to end hate and domestic violence, HIV-related violence, pickup crimes, rape, sexual assault, and other forms of violence affecting LGBT communities."
4. Perry Bacon Jr., "After 10-year dispute, expansion of hate crimes law to gays signed," *Washington Post*, October 29, 2009, Politics and The Nation section.
5. Andrew Kessinger, "Help Gays who aren't hurt," *Washington Post*, October 29, 2009.
6. *Weekly Gleaner*, October 16-22, 2008. The *Gleaner* is the island's leading newspaper.
7. *Weekly Gleaner*, March 12-18, 2009.
8. Jeannine Amber, "Trouble in Paradise," *Essence*, March 2009.

NOTES

Chapter 4

1. Kathy Obear, Ed.D. founding faculty, Social Justice Training Institute, www.sjti.org, managing partner, Alliance for Change Consultants, www.alliance-forchange.com, a training and organizational development consulting firm specializing in creating inclusion, team, and organizational effectiveness, conflict resolution, and change management.
2. Suzanne Pharr, *Homophobia: A Weapon of Sexism* (Chardon Press, 1988), 18.
3. Wishik and Pierce, *Sexual Orientation and Identity*.
4. *American Psychological Association.* (2008). Answers to your questions: For a better understanding of sexual orientation and homosexuality. Washington, DC: Retrieved from www.a.pa.org/topics/sorientation.pdf. Copyright© 2008 American Psychological Association.
5. Pharr, *Homophobia*, 18.
6. Adrienne Rich, "Foreword," in *The Coming Out Stories*, ed. Julia Penelope and Susan Wolfe (Watertown, MA: Persephone Press, 1979), xii; reprinted as *The Original Coming Out Stories* (Freedom, CA: Crossing Press, 1989). Source: Wishik and Pierce, *Sexual Orientation and Identity*.
7. Beth Brant, "Reclamation: A Lesbian Indian Story," in *Women-Identified Women* (Mayfield Publishing Company, 1984), 97. Source: Wishik and Pierce, *Sexual Orientation and Identity*.
8. Anthony R. D'Augelli, "Identity Development and Sexual Orientation: Toward a Model of Lesbian, Gay, and Bisexual Development," in *Human Diversity: Perspectives on People in Context*, ed. E.J. Trickett, R. Watts, and D. Berman (San Francisco: Jossey-Bass, 1994), 4-5. Source: Wishik and Pierce, Sexual Orientation and Identity.
9. Pharr, *Homophobia*.
10. Dana Milbank, "Washington Sketch," *Washington Post*, February 3, 2010.

THE AUTHOR

Shirley Anderson Fletcher has consulted to private corporations, government agencies and non-profit organizations for over thirty years. Her primary mission has been to assist clients in the United States and internationally to develop organizational cultures that value and support excellence in performance from all employees regardless of sexual orientation, national origin, culture, race, gender, age or other social identity.

She is an Applied Behavioral Scientist with a Masters Degree from Johns Hopkins University, a graduate Diploma in Education from Oxford University, and an Honors Degree in History from London University/University College of the West Indies.

Shirley is an accomplished organization systems analyst, executive coach and group facilitator. She has applied her expertise to companies in the pharmaceutical industry, banking, and the petroleum industry as well as public utilities. She is also an avid gardener, and crossword puzzle fanatic. She and her husband of forty-six years have two children and three grand children.

Shirley may be contacted at: shirley@danceofdifference.com

REVIEWS

"The book skillfully navigates an issue of prejudice and discrimination that is personal as it is public, experiential as it is conceptual and national as it is transnational. The methodology will appeal to various audiences, providing a "space" for critical reflection that is unsettling yet comforting, disturbing yet enlightening. Not only does the book contribute to the discourse on social oppression, but will prompt the reader to (re)consider how such oppression manifests itself in the various dimensions of real life experiences."

Dorith Grant-Wisdom, PhD., Political Scientist, University of Maryland

Reading this book is a remarkably powerful learning experience. Your writing provides one of the best examples of using "self" as a teaching tool for diversity and inclusion that I have experienced. You share deep insights in a caring, authentic and unselfish spirit of personal courage and unflinching honesty. This book certainly will move to the top of recommended readings for those pursuing their own diversity journeys and for those serious about building their skills in the work of diversity and inclusion. As a white, heterosexual man, it is at the top of my list.

R. Rushton Paul, Jr., SPHR
President, R. Rushton Paul Consulting, LLC - former HR Executive Wachovia

THE DANCE OF DIFFERENCE

This is an excellent read about a critical social justice topic for a population that continues to be treated oppressively around our world. The case studies at the end of the book make this especially useful for affinity groups, as part of diversity programs, teachers' education, and other types of consciousness-raising groups. The stories in this book — Shirley's and others that need telling are powerful and compelling as well as illustrative of the way cultures work.

AndreaZintz, Ph.D., President, Strategic Leadership Resources LLC

This book opened my eyes, and put a human face on gay and lesbian issues. Some of our friends and neighbors are in the LGBT community. However, we may not know it, and be unaware of the added challenges they face in everyday life. This book helps expand understanding of their situations, and stimulates thinking on how to be constructive and supportive.

E. H. Denton, Ph.D., Educator, Washington DC.

Anderson Fletcher's voice is authentic as it is courageous. Her decades of work as an Applied Behavioral Scientist specializing in Diversity - facilitates the process whereby the reader experiences the trauma of homophobia and the way it seeps into our Being and impacts our world. More importantly, because of the methodology of the book, she shares powerfully not only her own experience with us, but invites us to share ours through reflection and enquiry. The methodology of the book is critical for exploring not only sexual orientation but is applicable to any area of discrimination. Anderson Fletcher points out that all are inextricably linked.

Beverley Anderson Manley, Broadcaster, Political Scientist, former First Lady of Jamaica

Made in the USA
Lexington, KY
22 June 2011